MINUTES of MEETINGS

of the

COMBINED CHIEFS OF STAFF

POST-ARCADIA

VOLUME I

Recorded and printed in the
Office of the Combined Chiefs of Staff
Washington, D. C.

1942

Published by Books Express Publishing
Copyright © Books Express, 2011
ISBN 978-1-780393-96-4

Books Express publications are available from all good retail and online booksellers. For publishing proposals and direct ordering please contact us at: info@books-express.com

TABLE OF CONTENTS
TWENTY MEETINGS OF THE COMBINED CHIEFS OF STAFF
JANUARY 23rd, 1942, to MAY 19th, 1942.

MEETING MINUTES *PAGE NUMBER*

1st	1
2nd	12
3rd	22
4th	33
5th	42
6th	52
7th	56
8th	60
9th	69
10th	76
11th	85
12th	91
13th	101
14th	111
15th	119
16th	127
17th	134
18th	142
19th	147
20th	152
Index	I-XIV

U. S. SECRET
BRITISH MOST SECRET

C.C.S. 1st Meeting

COMBINED CHIEFS OF STAFF

MINUTES of a Meeting held in Room 1202, Federal Reserve Building, on Friday, January 23, 1942, at 3:00 p.m.

PRESENT

Admiral H. R. Stark, USN
General G. C. Marshall, USA
Admiral E. J. King, USN
Lt. General H.H. Arnold, USA

Field Marshal Sir John Dill
Admiral Sir Charles Little
Lt.General Sir Colville Wemyss
Group Captain S. C. Strafford
(representing Air Marshal Harris)

THE FOLLOWING WERE ALSO PRESENT

Rear Admiral R. K. Turner, USN
Brig. General L. T. Gerow, USA
Rear Admiral J. H. Towers, USN
Captain F. C. Denebrink, USN
Commander R. E. Libby, USN

Captain C. E. Lambe, RN

SECRETARIAT

Brigadier V. Dykes
Commander L.R. McDowell, USN
Commander R.D. Coleridge, RN

U. S. SECRET
BRITISH MOST SECRET

1. GENERAL WAVELL'S APPRECIATION OF SITUATION IN ABDA AREA.
   (ABDACOM 00053 of January 15, 1942)

GENERAL MARSHALL read to the Committee a document containing the comments of the U.S. War Department on General Wavell's Appreciation.

A convoy containing 22,000 U.S. reinforcements had sailed that day. It was hoped that these reinforcements would arrive in Australia on February 20. With regard to supplies for the Philippines, which were short of A.A. ammunition and rations, U.S. officers were endeavoring to buy up local craft in order to break the Japanese blockade, thereby providing supplies and encouragement to the Philippine garrison.

ADMIRAL KING mentioned that he had that day seen Mr. Casey, who had stated that, in his opinion, the Australian Government would be unable to provide any relief for the United States garrison which was being sent to New Caledonia.

SIR JOHN DILL explained the Australian position with regard to man-power, and stated that they had only 130,000 troops to protect the whole of the Australian Continent. Australia was undoubtedly fearful of Japanese raids, and Mr. Casey had asked him to take action to provide tanks for Australia; to which he had replied that the Australian requirement could not be dealt with as an isolated case, and must be considered in conjunction with our many other commitments.

SIR JOHN DILL then mentioned the question of Timor. The Portuguese had agreed to Staff discussions, but were anxious to undertake the garrisoning of their own half of the island.

He asked General Marshall if he were satisfied with General Wavell's arrangement, whereby General Brett was in charge of the administration. He himself had been inclined to feel that General Brett should not be asked to shoulder this responsibility, in view of his important task as Deputy Commander.

U. S. SECRET
BRITISH MOST SECRET

GENERAL MARSHALL said that he had taken the same view himself, but was loath to interfere with General Wavell's arrangements, in view of the difficulty he must be experiencing in initiating his command.

THE COMMITTEE:

Took note that a despatch had been sent by General Marshall to General Brett through General Wavell, containing the main points of the Memorandum read to the Committee by General Marshall.

2. NAVAL REINFORCEMENTS FOR ABDA AREA.
   (a) C.C.S. 2; ABDACOM 00053, para. 11(a).
   (b) C.C.S. 2/1.
   (c) ABDACOM 00235 of January 22.
   (d) ABDACOM 00200 of January 21.
   (e) C.C.S. 7.

With regard to reference (d) above, Admiral King said that he felt there must be some misapprehension with regard to U.S. Naval forces in the Area. These consisted of 3 Cruisers, 13 Destroyers, 3 Gunboats, and other small craft.

ADMIRAL LITTLE said that he realized that the Naval forces in the ABDA Area must be considered in conjunction with those allocated to the ANZAC Area; and in this connection he drew the attention of the Committee to C.C.S. 7 which contained a telegram from the Government of Australia to the Prime Minister.

ADMIRAL KING pointed out that this telegram purported to lay down the tasks of the Commander in Chief, U.S. Pacific Fleet. The ANZAC Area was merely an adjunct to the Pacific Command. The responsibility for the safe escort of convoys arriving in Australia from the westward lay either with the ABDA Command or with the Commander in Chief, Eastern Fleet. Mr. Casey had expressed surprise when he had suggested to him that forces in the ANZAC Area would escort U.S. convoys through that

U. S. SECRET
BRITISH MOST SECRET

Area to Australia.

ADMIRAL LITTLE said that in discussions during the recent Conferences, when the question of building up Australia as a base for future operations had been discussed, he had had the impression that units of the Pacific Fleet would escort westbound convoys right through to Australia.

ADMIRAL KING stated that this had not been his impression, and it would be difficult, in view of the many commitments of the U.S. Pacific Fleet. Naval reinforcements for the ABDA Area must, however, be reconsidered, in order that the best possible use could be made of the available forces.

ADMIRAL LITTLE stated that the British Chiefs of Staff had commented on the Australian telegram contained in C.C.S. 7, in two respects. First, they had suggested that the U.S. Commander in the ANZAC Area should be situated ashore at Melbourne, in order that he would be in close contact with the Australian Commonwealth Naval Board on the subject of convoys; and secondly, that as the command of the Commander in Chief, Eastern Fleet, would extend to the western limit of the ABDA Area, and on the South and West of Australia to the western limit of the ANZAC Area, it would be necessary for the provision of escorts for convoys proceeding to the ABDA Area to be arranged between the Commander in Chief, Eastern Fleet, and the Naval Commanders in the ANZAC and ABDA Areas.

ADMIRAL KING expressed his agreement with both the above points.

THE COMMITTEE was informed that a telegram had just arrived from London, giving the British ships allocated to the ABDA Area.

THE COMMITTEE:-

    (a) Instructed the Secretaries to circulate a Memorandum* showing the British Naval forces stationed

U. S. SECRET
BRITISH MOST SECRET

                in the ABDA AREA.

        (b) Agreed to reconsider the question of Naval reinforcements for the ABDA Area at their next meeting.

*Subsequently circulated as C.C.S. 10.

3.   SITUATION IN PHILLIPPINE AREA.
       (ABDACOM 00100 of January 17, 1942)

GENERAL MARSHALL read to the Committee a telegram which he had received from General MacArthur containing extracts from a telegram to General MacArthur from General Wavell giving his appreciation of the general situation and containing a suggestion that he (General Wavell) should visit General MacArthur. General MacArthur had begged General Wavell not to undertake this hazardous journey.

With regard to paragraph 8 of ABDACOM 00100, the U.S. Chiefs of Staff were considering the possibility of getting further supplies into Mindanao, and would draft a reply to that part of General Wavell's message.

ADMIRAL KING said that in addition to the action outlined by General Marshall with regard to small native vessels for running the blockade, he had instructed Admiral Hart, prior to General Wavell's assumption of command, to send 2 submarines with .50 caliber and A.A. ammunition to the Philippines. A further submarine had been despatched from Hawaii on January 12 with supplies of 3-inch ammunition. The estimated length of the passage was 22 days, and Admiral Hart had been informed of this action.

THE COMMITTEE:-

Took note that the U.S. Chiefs of Staff would prepare a draft reply to paragraph 8 of ABDACOM 00100.

U. S. SECRET
BRITISH MOST SECRET

4. EMPLOYMENT OF A.V.G. IN BURMA AND CHINA.
   (C.C.S. 4)

The U.S. Chiefs of Staff presented a memorandum on the subject of the proposed amendments to C.C.S. 4.

GENERAL MARSHALL explained that General Magruder was under the direct control of Generalissimo Chiang Kai-Shek. He felt it essential to retain the phrase "on call from Chiang Kai-Shek" in the penultimate sentence of paragraph (b) of the draft contained in C.C.S. 4. This he thought was important for political reasons and in order not to discourage Chiang Kai-Shek.

SIR JOHN DILL suggested the substitution of the words "The operations" for "his control" in the latter half of the second sentence of paragraph (b). He further suggested that a personal telegram should be despatched from the U.S. Chiefs of Staff to General Magruder explaining that, in spite of the fact that American forces despatched to Burma must be returned to Generalissimo Chiang Kai-Shek "on call from him," yet this should only be done after due notice had been given to General Wavell.

THE COMMITTEE:-

(a) Instructed the Secretaries to despatch the telegram to General Wavell as amended in the course of discussion*.

(b) Took note that General Marshall would despatch a personal telegram to General Magruder on the lines suggested by Sir John Dill.

(c) Instructed the Secretaries to inform General Wavell of the terms of the personal message to General Magruder.

*Subsequently despatched as D.B.A. 1

U. S. SECRET
BRITISH MOST SECRET

5. SUPER GYMNAST
   (a) C.C.S. 5/1

THE COMMITTEE was informed that the first line of the enclosure to C.C.S. 5/1 should read "U.S. Navy Combat Loaded Ships."

ADMIRAL STARK and GENERAL MARSHALL stressed the present shortage of U.S. shipping.

GENERAL MARSHALL said that Admiral Land had reported a present shortage of 92 ships. While it had been agreed that the reinforcements to the Far East should be expedited, the President and Prime Minister had given a ruling that this should entail no stoppage of supplies to Russia or the Middle East. The only method of obtaining additional ships appeared to be to request the President and the Prime Minister to approve of the use of the special combat loaded ships detailed for modified Super Gymnast. This would have the effect of postponing D date for this Operation until about March 20.

SIR JOHN DILL mentioned the risk of losing this valuable type of special ship if they were employed in conveying U.S. troops to Northern Ireland.

ADMIRAL KING said that there were additional points to be remembered, such as the U.S. inability to undertake the shipping of troops to northeast Brazil, and also the fact that if these ships were used in the North Atlantic all training of the Amphibious force would of necessity be stopped.

THE COMMITTEE:-

Instructed the Combined Staff Planners to prepare a memorandum for the Combined Chiefs of Staff setting out the implications of the proposal contained in C.C.S. 5/1.

U. S. SECRET
BRITISH MOST SECRET

5. (b) C.C.S. 5.

THE COMMITTEE considered the draft terms of reference of the Combined Staff Planners contained in C.C.S. 5.

ADMIRAL KING pointed out that if it were decided to use the U.S. combat loaded ships for Operation "Magnet," the earliest date at which modified Super Gymnast could be undertaken would be about March 20.

THE COMMITTEE:-

Agreed that the terms of reference contained in C.C.S. 5 should be remitted to the Combined Staff Planners as their directive.

6. CHANGE IN WESTERN ATLANTIC AREA AS DEFINED IN ABC-1.
(C.C.S. 1)

ADMIRAL KING stated that he had hopes that the Rio de Janeiro Conference might achieve some arrangement whereby the Brazilians, Argentines and Uruguayans would undertake naval patrolling duties off their own coasts thereby freeing U.S. and British ships for other duties. He was anxious, therefore, that no alteration at present should be made in the existing arrangements for the dividing line in the Atlantic.

THE COMMITTEE:-

Agreed that the division of responsibility in the Atlantic should remain as at present, pending further consideration in the light of the results of the Rio de Janeiro Conference.

7. FREE FRENCH FORCES IN THE PACIFIC.
(C.C.S. 6)

ADMIRAL LITTLE informed the Committee that the New Zealand Government had made representations that they should be relieved of the

U. S. SECRET
BRITISH MOST SECRET

responsibility for assisting in the defense of Tahiti. It was hoped to present a memorandum to the Combined Chiefs of Staff on this subject shortly.

    THE COMMITTEE:-

    Agreed that consideration of the approach by the Free French, contained in the enclosure to C.C.S. 6, should be deferred for the present.

8.   U.S. TRANSPORTS IN THE INDIAN OCEAN.
    (C.C.S. 3)

    THE COMMITTEE:-

    Took note of the above paper.

9.   POST ARCADIA COLLABORATION.
    (W.W. 16)

    ADMIRAL KING said that W.W. 16, as agreed by the Combined Chiefs of Staff, had not yet received the approval of the President or Prime Minister. He felt that before presenting it for approval, certain revisions should be made to it. It seemed unnecessary that individuals should be mentioned by name, and the wording of paragraph 5 whereby the Combined Chiefs of Staff in Washington were responsible only by implication for areas other than the ABDA Area, should be reworded.

    THE COMMITTEE:-

    Instructed the Combined Staff Planners to prepare a redraft of W.W. 16 for consideration by the Combined Chiefs of Staff prior to its being laid before the President and Prime Minister.

U. S. SECRET
BRITISH MOST SECRET

10. SUPPLIES FOR THE DUTCH IN THE ABDA AREA.

GENERAL ARNOLD said that he was continuing to receive direct requests from the Dutch for supplies, such as bombs, for their aircraft operating in the ABDA Area.

GENERAL MARSHALL said that the Lieutenant Governor of the Netherlands East Indies had been to see him and appeared worried on the subject of allocation of material to the Netherlands East Indies forces. The Lieutenant Governor was not satisfied that the Dutch Government in London was in a position to handle the matter of allocations, and was anxious that it should be centralized in Washington.

THE COMMITTEE:

Agreed that material arriving in the ABDA Area should be considered as available for use by any of the United Nations and should be allocated in accordance with strategic needs by General Wavell who would issue the necessary directions to General Brett, his Intendant General.

11. DESPATCHES TO GENERAL BRETT.

GENERAL MARSHALL said that there were many subjects, such as the establishment of U.S. bases in Australia, with which he had to deal direct with General Brett. In order, however, that General Wavell should not be short-circuited, he was sending these telegrams from himself personally to General Wavell for General Brett.

Copies of these messages would in future be sent to the Representatives of the British Chiefs of Staff.

THE COMMITTEE:

Took note of the above statement.

U. S. SECRET
BRITISH MOST SECRET

12. INFORMATION FROM THE ABDA AREA.

SIR JOHN DILL said that he had sent a personal telegram to General Wavell, reminding him of the necessity for keeping the Combined Chiefs of Staff in Washington fully informed of the situation, and of his plans.

THE COMMITTEE:-

Took note of the above statement.

13. NEXT MEETING.

The Committee agreed to meet at 3 p.m. on Monday, January 26, 1942, in the Federal Reserve Building.

U. S. SECRET
BRITISH MOST SECRET

C.C.S. 2nd Meeting

COMBINED CHIEFS OF STAFF

MINUTES of a Meeting held in Room 2907,
Navy Department, on Tuesday, January 27, 1942,
at 3:00 p.m.

PRESENT

Admiral H. R. Stark, USN
General G. C. Marshall, USA
Admiral E. J. King, USN
Lt. General H.H. Arnold, USA

Field Marshal Sir John Dill
Admiral Sir Charles Little
Lt. General Sir Colville Wemyss
Air Marshal A. T. Harris

THE FOLLOWING WERE ALSO PRESENT

Rear Admiral R.K. Turner, USN
Rear Admiral J.H. Towers, USN
Brig. General L.T. Gerow, USA
Captain F. C. Denebrink, USN
Commander R. E. Libby, USN

Captain C. E. Lambe, RN
Captain G.D. Belben, RN

SECRETARIAT

Brigadier V. Dykes
Commander L. R. McDowell, USN
Commander R. D. Coleridge, RN

U. S. SECRET
BRITISH MOST SECRET

1. NAVAL REINFORCEMENTS FOR THE ABDA AREA.
   (C.C.S.2, C.C.S. 2/1, ABDACOM 00235 of January 22, 1942, ABDACOM 00200 of January 21, 1942, and C.C.S. 10).

   After a short discussion -

   THE COMMITTEE:-

   Agreed to defer consideration of the question of naval reinforcements for the ABDA Area until a satisfactory solution had been reached over the ANZAC Area.

2. ANZAC AREA.
   (C.C.S. 7)

   ADMIRAL KING said that he had discussed the question of the ANZAC Area at considerable length with Admiral Little, and as a result certain proposals had been referred to all the parties concerned. The Australian Government had raised two points which still had to be settled. First, they wished to retain one cruiser in the ANZAC Area until H.M.A.S. "CANBERRA" had been repaired, and second, they wished to keep 8 anti-submarine craft under their own control for the protection of coastal convoys instead of allotting them to the ANZAC Area. If these vessels were retained, there would only be two Australian and two U.S. destroyers at the disposal of the Admiral in Command of the ANZAC Area. In his view it would be a far more satisfactory solution to place the whole responsibility on the Commander of the ANZAC Area. The ships in question could operate under a suitable subordinate commander. This would be a much more flexible arrangement. On the question of the cruiser, he felt that it was a very unsound principle that the ANZAC Area should not take its fair share of deficiencies due to ships being under repair. These deficiencies must occur in every area and each Commander in Chief had to make the best dispositions possible in the circumstances.

   ADMIRAL LITTLE said that the Australian Commonwealth Naval Board was probably under the impression that coastal convoys would be their responsibility, and if they were relieved of this it seemed quite

U. S. SECRET
BRITISH MOST SECRET

likely that they would accept Admiral King's proposal regarding the 8 anti-submarine vessels.

THE COMMITTEE:-

Took note that the matter would be further discussed between Admiral King and Admiral Little, who would draw up in consultation the necessary telegrams to the various authorities concerned, and despatch them in the names of the Combined Chiefs of Staff.

3. MODIFIED SUPER GYMNAST.
   (C.C.S. 5/1 and C.C.S. 11)

   THE COMMITTEE:-

   (a) Took note of a report by the Combined Staff Planners (C.C.S. 11) on the implications of employing the U.S. Navy combat loaded ships and accompanying cargo vessels for the movement of one convoy of troops to Northern Ireland.

   (b) Took note that the Representatives of the British Chiefs of Staff, in view of the political implications, would refer the proposal to London and obtain the views of the Prime Minister prior to the submission of the proposal by the U.S. Chiefs of Staff to the President.

4. SUPPORT OF CHIANG KAI-SHEK.
   (C.C.S. 13)

SIR JOHN DILL said that, since the draft telegram to General Wavell, which was under discussion, had been drafted, a telegram had been received from London saying that General Wavell had been asked to keep Chiang Kai-Shek fully informed of the situation in the ABDA Area through the British Military Attache at Chungking. It was hoped that, by

U. S. SECRET
BRITISH MOST SECRET

this means, any resentment on the part of Chiang Kai-Shek at his being kept in the dark on the war situation would be removed. In these circumstances he suggested that any further telegram to General Wavell was unnecessary.

    THE COMMITTEE:-

Agreed that in the circumstances the proposed telegram should not be despatched.

5.   DEFENSE OF TAHITI.
      (C.C.S. 12)

    THE COMMITTEE had under consideration a memorandum by the Representatives of the British Chiefs of Staff on the Defense of Tahiti (C.C.S. 12).

    ADMIRAL KING said that the U.S. Forces would shortly be established in the Society Islands at Bora Bora. In these circumstances he saw no objection to an announcement in general terms of the intention of the U.S. to relieve the New Zealand Government of their responsibility for assistance to these Free French possessions.

    ADMIRAL STARK said that it would be undesirable to make any announcement of the details of the U.S. forces which were being sent until after they were fully established.

    THE COMMITTEE AGREED:-

        (a) To recommend to the President and to the Prime Minister that a public announcement should be made to the effect that the U.S. had relieved the New Zealand Government of the responsibility for providing assistance to the Free French Colonies in the Society Islands, in the event of attack.

U. S. SECRET
BRITISH MOST SECRET

5.   (b) That the Representatives of the British Chiefs of Staff should arrange for a draft announcement on these lines to be telegraphed from London to the President for his approval before publication.

6. INCLUSION OF DARWIN IN THE ABDA AREA.
(C.C.S. 8 and D.B.A. No. 2 to ABDACOM)

THE COMMITTEE:-

Took note that D.B.A. No. 2 had been despatched from the Combined Chiefs of Staff to General Wavell.

7. SUPPLIES FOR THE DUTCH IN THE ABDA AREA.
(Previous Reference: C.C.S. 1st Meeting, Item 10)

ADMIRAL STARK presented a draft telegram from the Combined Chiefs of Staff to General Wavell, resulting from the representations of the Lieutenant-Governor of the Dutch East Indies (Van Mook).

AIR MARSHAL HARRIS suggested that before sending aircraft to be operated by Dutch personnel, it would be essential for General Brett to make sure that the Dutch had the necessary fully trained pilots and ground organization.

THE COMMITTEE:-

Took note that the Representatives of the British Chiefs of Staff would further study this telegram, and inform the U.S. Chiefs of Staff as soon as possible as to their agreement, or otherwise, with the terms of it.

8. MALAYA AND NEW GUINEA SITUATION.
(C.C.S. 14)

GENERAL MARSHALL explained that the telegram contained as an enclosure to C.C.S. 14 had been despatched by the Prime Minister of Aus-

U. S. SECRET
BRITISH MOST SECRET

tralia to the Prime Minister of Great Britain on January 23, 1942, and a copy of it had been given to the President by Mr. Casey. The President had instructed the Combined Chiefs of Staff to study this telegram.

THE COMMITTEE agreed that Parts 1 and 2 of the telegram were of a political nature, to which the Prime Minister would undoubtedly be replying direct to the Prime Minister of Australia.

GENERAL MARSHALL then read to the Committee a telegram, not completely decipherable, from General Brett containing a message from General Brereton in Australia commenting on the unsatisfactory state of Australian defenses, and the necessity for some form of unified command in Australia.

GENERAL ARNOLD suggested that perhaps the extension of the ABDA Area already agreed to did not go far enough. The Southern Celebes and New Guinea contained bases from which the Japanese could attack both Darwin and Timor. The inclusion of the Northeastern peninsula of Australia within the responsibility of General Wavell would allow him to base aircraft there, and might thus render it unnecessary to divert fighters to the Australians.

SIR JOHN DILL said that by the terms of his Directive, General Wavell was allowed to operate forces outside his own Area, and could therefore, should he see fit, make use of bases in the Northeastern peninsula of Australia. He doubted the wisdom of increasing the coastal frontiers of General Wavell's command.

GENERAL MARSHALL pointed out that when the planned aircraft reinforcements to the ABDA Area had arrived, there could be no new shipment of fighter aircraft to either the ABDA Area or Australia for two months. Anything that was given to Australia must of necessity be at the expense of the ABDA Area.

SIR JOHN DILL pointed out that in view of the importance of General Wavell's lines of communication to him, he might see fit, whether it were included in his Area or not, to base some of his fighter

U. S. SECRET
BRITISH MOST SECRET

aircraft in the Northeastern peninsula of Australia.

GENERAL ARNOLD suggested that the Australian request might be referred to General Wavell; at the same time it being explained to him that no additional aircraft other than those already assigned to his Area could be forthcoming, for at least two months.

SIR JOHN DILL welcomed this proposal, but pointed out that the terms of this telegram would have to be referred to the Prime Minister in view of the fact that the original telegram had been addressed to him by the Prime Minister of Australia.

THE COMMITTEE:--

(a) Took note that the U.S. Chiefs of Staff would prepare a draft telegram to General Wavell, informing him of the Australian request for fighter aircraft, and that no additional aircraft other than those assigned to himself were available; and asking him to take such action as he might see fit.

(b) Took note that this draft telegram would be referred to the British Chiefs of Staff and the Prime Minister before its despatch by the Combined Chiefs of Staff.

9. EMPLOYMENT OF A.V.G. IN BURMA AND CHINA.
(ABDACOM W. 2/00357 of January 26, 1942)

SIR JOHN DILL referred to the request contained in W. 2 dated January 26, 1942, from General Wavell, that he might be informed under whose orders the A.V.G. Squadron was to be regarded as operating. As this telegram had crossed the Combined Chiefs' of Staff telegram D.B.A. No. 1, which explained the position with regard to the U.S. forces in China and Burma, he felt that no answer was now required.

He then drew attention to a telegram received from the British

U. S. SECRET
BRITISH MOST SECRET

Chiefs of Staff, saying that Burma had reported that all A.V.G. units would be withdrawn by January 31, 1942, on account of continued loss. As this withdrawal would leave Rangoon defended only by 2 Hurricanes and 4 Buffaloes, the Chiefs of Staff had requested that this matter should be taken up with the U.S. Chiefs of Staff, and that the A.V.G. should remain at Rangoon pending the arrival of 36 Hurricanes which would arrive there by February 1, 1942.

GENERAL ARNOLD explained that in an effort to speed up the reinforcements to the A.V.G., 51 aircraft were going to be erected at Takoradi, and flown across. It was a difficult flight, and the serviceability of those which arrived would not be high. He also mentioned the recent attack on Fort Lamy, which form of attack, if continued, might jeopardize the Takoradi route.

THE COMMITTEE:-

(a) Took note that General Marshall would despatch a telegram to General Magruder for Generalissimo Chiang Kai-Shek, reminding him of the importance of Rangoon as the port of entry for all his supplies, and informing him that the Combined Chiefs of Staff hoped that the A.V.G. unit could be retained at Rangoon until the arrival of the 36 British Hurricanes on February 1, 1942.

(b) Took note that General Marshall would send a personal telegram to General Wavell, informing him of the action he had taken with Generalissimo Chiang Kai-Shek.

10. RUSSIAN ATTITUDE TO JAPAN.
(ABDACOM 00278 of January 23, 1942)

SIR JOHN DILL drew attention to the above telegram from General Wavell suggesting that the Russians should be urged to take steps to keep the Japanese forces in Manchuria in constant apprehension of

U. S. SECRET
BRITISH MOST SECRET

attack. He felt that this matter was political and diplomatic rather than one for the Combined Chiefs of Staff.

GENERAL MARSHALL said that successful defense of our Far Eastern position was likely to weigh far more with the Russians than any diplomatic approach at this state. There had recently been violent remonstrances from the Russians on what they considered to be a breach of faith in that the complete equipment promised at the Moscow Protocol had not been forthcoming.

THE COMMITTEE:-

Agreed that no action on ABDACOM 00278 should be taken by the Combined Chiefs of Staff.

11.   ALLOCATION OF UNITED STATES HEAVY BOMBARDMENT GROUPS.

GENERAL ARNOLD said that in the recent discussions, Air-Chief Marshal Portal had asked that 20 United States Heavy Bombardment Groups should be operating from the United Kingdom by December 1942. It now appeared that 16 Groups would be available for use outside the United States by that date, but the ground forces to maintain them would amount to approximately 80,000 men and it would be necessary to consider the shipping problem resulting from the necessary maintenance of these 16 Groups overseas.

Both Admiral King and Sir John Dill felt that it was too early at this state to reach a decision as to the best area in which these 16 Heavy Bombardment Groups should operate. It might be better to send certain of them to the Far East.

ADMIRAL KING said that apart from purely strategical considerations it was obviously necessary for political reasons, in order to stress solidarity of purpose between the United Nations, that at least certain of these aircraft should operate from bases in the United Kingdom at the earliest possible date.

U. S. SECRET
BRITISH MOST SECRET

GENERAL ARNOLD said that a decision as to the employment of the Bombardment Groups was required well in advance, in order that the necessary ground facilities should be provided beforehand.

THE COMMITTEE:-

(a) Agreed that the first two United States Heavy Bombardment Groups should be assigned for operations from United Kingdom bases.

(b) Instructed the Combined Staff Planners to study and report on the arrangements for this move.

(c) Agreed to defer consideration of the allocation of the remaining 14 Heavy Bombardment Groups for a later date.

12. NEXT MEETING.

THE COMMITTEE:-

Agreed, that unless urgent business necessitated an earlier meeting, to meet at 3:00 p.m. on Tuesday, February 3, 1942, in Room 2907 in the Navy Department.

U. S. SECRET
BRITISH MOST SECRET

C.C.S. 3rd Meeting

COMBINED CHIEFS OF STAFF

MINUTES of a Meeting held in Room 340,
Public Health Building, on Tuesday, February
3, 1942, at 3:00 p.m.

PRESENT

Admiral H. R. Stark, USN	Field Marshal Sir John Dill
General G. C. Marshall, USA	Admiral Sir Charles Little
Admiral E. J. King, USN	Lt. General Sir Colville Wemyss
Lt. General H.H. Arnold, USA	Air Marshal A. T. Harris

THE FOLLOWING WERE ALSO PRESENT

Rear Admiral J.H. Towers, USN
Rear Admiral R.K. Turner, USN
Brig. General L.T. Gerow, USA
Captain F. C. Denebrink, USN
Commander R. E. Libby, USN
Lt. Colonel E. L. Sibert, USA

Air Marshal D. C. S. Evill
Captain G. D. Belben, RN
Group Captain S.C. Strafford

For Item 8:
R. Adm. J.E.M. Ranneft, RNN,
  Dutch Naval Attache
Col. F.G.L. Weijerman, RNIA
  Dutch Military Attache
H. E. Dr. H. Van Mook,
  Lieutenant-Governor, NEI

SECRETARIAT

Brigadier V. Dykes
Brig. Gen. W.B. Smith, USA
Commander L.R. McDowell, USN
Commander R.D. Coleridge, RN

U. S. SECRET
BRITISH MOST SECRET

1. U. S. NAVAL OPERATIONS IN THE WESTERN PACIFIC.

SIR JOHN DILL offered the congratulations of the Representatives of the British Chiefs of Staff to Admiral Stark and Admiral King on the successful U.S. naval operations in the Japanese mandated islands.

2. CABLE SHIP "J.W. MACKAY."

ADMIRAL LITTLE, on behalf of Sir Dudley Pound, thanked Admiral Stark for releasing this ship for important work in the Indian Ocean.

3. NAVAL REINFORCEMENTS FOR THE ABDA AREA.
   (Previous Reference: C.C.S. 2nd Meeting, Minute 1, C.C.S. 2, 2/1, 10; ABDACOMS 00235 of 22/1 and 00200 of 21/1)

ADMIRAL KING said that since the institution of the ANZAC Area, the ABDA Area had been reinforced by 2 Light Cruisers, 2 Destroyers, and 3 Sloops from Australia. One further British Cruiser might be made available if, as a result of satisfactory negotiations with the South American Republics, British ships could be released from the east coast of South America.

ADMIRAL LITTLE said that Sir Dudley Pound did not at present intend withdrawing the four modern destroyers from the ABDA Area.

THE COMMITTEE:-

Took note of the above statements.

4. REPRESENTATION OF THE BRITISH DOMINIONS AND DUTCH.
   (C.C.S. 21)

SIR JOHN DILL said he had had a telegram from the Prime Minister, asking him to delay a decision on this matter pending the result of his approaches to the Australian and New Zealand Governments.

U. S. SECRET
BRITISH MOST SECRET

ADMIRAL STARK said that he was most anxious to have some form of review of the matter by the Combined Chiefs of Staff available for the President at short notice.

ADMIRAL KING stressed the necessity for finally approving the revised Charter for the Combined Chiefs of Staff at an early date.

THE COMMITTEE then considered C.C.S. 21, and made certain amendments to it.

THE COMMITTEE:-

Instructed the Secretaries to circulate the enclosure to C.C.S. 21, as amended in the course of discussion, as a Memorandum* by the Combined Chiefs of Staff.

*Subsequently circulated as C.C.S. 21/1.

5. RELATIONS WITH VICHY FRANCE.

GENERAL GEROW outlined a conversation he had had with Mr. Hull.

Admiral Muselier's coup d'etat in St. Pierre and Miquelon, and General Rommel's recent counter attack in Libya had stiffened the Vichy attitude. Information from secret sources suggested that unless there was a return to the status quo in St. Pierre and Miquelon, Vichy might not only eject U.S. Consuls and Observers in France and North Africa, but also collaborate with the Japanese in regard to New Caledonia. Mr. Hull feared that Vichy might go so far as to turn over the Fleet and bases to the Germans. He was most anxious that the Combined Chiefs of Staff should give an opinion as to the military dangers of further Vichy collaboration with Germany, in order that the British Government might be urged to take further action to restore the status quo in St. Pierre and Miquelon.

SIR JOHN DILL agreed with the importance of retaining rela-

U. S. SECRET
BRITISH MOST SECRET

tions with Vichy France, particularly in view of the danger of the French Fleet and bases being turned over to the Germans, as well as losing important information should the Consuls and Observers be ejected.

THE COMMITTEE:-

(a) Agreed that with reference to the crisis which had arisen in the relations of Great Britain and the United States with the Vichy Government over the occupation of St. Pierre and Miquelon, the situation was exceedingly grave in its possible military consequences, and that a further determined effort should be made to adjust the present differences, in order that existing relations between the United States and Vichy France might be maintained.

(b) Invited Sir John Dill to represent the views of the Combined Chiefs of Staff, as set out above, to H.E. the British Ambassador.

6. POSSIBLE JAPANESE ACTION AGAINST AUSTRALIA AND NEW ZEALAND. (C.C.S. 18)

SIR JOHN DILL felt that this Appreciation could be improved, and that it took too narrow a view of the situation.

ADMIRAL STARK said that it was at present being considered by the Joint U.S. Intelligence Committee, and that he would prefer to defer a full discussion on it.

After discussion, THE COMMITTEE:-

Agreed that the Appreciation contained in C.C.S. 18, together with the comments and criticisms of the Joint U.S. Intelligence Committee, should be considered, and reported on by the Combined Staff Planners.

U. S. SECRET
BRITISH MOST SECRET

7. DEFENSE OF N.E. APPROACHES TO AUSTRALIA.

(Previous Reference: C.C.S. 2nd Meeting, Minute 8, D.B.A. 4, 5, and 7; ABDACOM 00649)

SIR JOHN DILL said that he felt it essential that as the responsibility for the allotment of forces to the ABDA and ANZAC Areas lay with the Combined Chiefs of Staff, they should have before them a full picture of the forces at present in the Area, en route for the Area, and of reinforcements projected during the next three months.

GENERAL ARNOLD then informed the Committee of the U.S. air reinforcements now in the Area, in passage, or projected.

AIR MARSHAL HARRIS said that with regard to the Australian and New Zealand requests for fighter aircraft, the British Chiefs of Staff were proposing to allocate 125 Kittyhawks to Australia and 18 to New Zealand within the next three months. This was based on the assumption that two U.S. pursuit groups would reach Egypt in April. He felt that these, and other ad hoc requests, could be dealt with only if the Combined Chiefs of Staff had before them a complete picture of the planned reinforcements of the ABDA and ANZAC Areas.

GENERAL MARSHALL said he regretted that General Wavell had not felt able, in view of his many other commitments, to take over the defense of N.E. Australia, but that as the successful defense of this Area was so vital to the lines of communication to the ABDA Area, he suggested that an allotment of fighters should be made to the Royal Australian Air Force from those fighters now in Australia which had been previously intended for the ABDA Area.

GENERAL MARSHALL then presented a draft telegram to General Wavell.

THE COMMITTEE:-

(a) Instructed the Combined Staff Planners, as a matter

U. S. SECRET
BRITISH MOST SECRET

of urgency, to draw up a comprehensive statement with respect to the ABDA and ANZAC Areas, and of Australia and New Zealand, showing the Naval, Air, and Land forces of the United Nations in or assigned to these Areas, under the following headings:-

(1) Forces at present in the Areas.

(2) Forces en route for the Areas.

(3) Reinforcements projected during the next three months.

(Reallocation of forces between Areas which may shortly become necessary, or at present under discussion, should not be taken into account.)

(b) Instructed the Secretaries to despatch to General Wavell the draft telegram* presented by General Marshall, as amended in the course of discussion.

*Subsequently despatched as D.B.A. 8.

(At this point, H.E. Dr. Van Mook, Lieutenant Governor of the Netherlands East Indies, R. Adm. Ranneft and Colonel Weijerman entered the meeting.)

8. REVIEW OF THE SITUATION IN THE ABDA AREA.

SIR JOHN DILL outlined the course of the war, and the present strategic situation. He then dealt in some detail with the situation in the ABDA Area.

DR. VAN MOOK thanked Sir John Dill for his explanation of the situation. He had been most anxious to meet the Combined Chiefs of Staff as, while the responsibility for the employment of the available forces in the ABDA Area rested with General Wavell, the forces to be allocated

U. S. SECRET
BRITISH MOST SECRET

to the Area were the responsibility of the Combined Chiefs of Staff. He realized that the defense of the Netherlands East Indies was only part of a much wider problem.

There were two particular points he wished to raise. First, he felt that the drive to Singapore would not end with the investment of the island, and if the Japanese isolated Singapore and could with reasonable safety move South, he wished to stress the value of the islands of Banka and Billiton as possessing the only remaining tin in the Area, and of Palembang, the largest oilfield in the Netherlands East Indies, possessing a large refinery which was the only one capable of producing high octane spirit.

Secondly, he felt that the United Nations should concentrate on Japanese communications, which were their main weakness. He considered that they should be attacked not only by air and submarines, but also by a striking force of surface vessels. The success achieved against the Japanese convoy in the Macassar Strait, which was not very strongly escorted, might have been far greater had a stronger surface striking force been available to us.

GENERAL ARNOLD and AIR MARSHAL HARRIS then outlined the air forces available, and en route to the Area from U.S. and British resources.

With regard to the Naval striking force, ADMIRAL KING said that the Cruiser PHOENIX had been sent to replace the BOISE, though this could not be taken as a precedent that all ships lost or damaged in the ABDA Area could be replaced. He hoped to send a further six small submarines to the ABDA Area.

ADMIRAL LITTLE explained that the Naval forces of the United Nations had to keep open the sea communications of the world. From this task there were at present no forces available to be diverted to the new theater of war. Production of new ships was a far longer process than the production of aircraft or Army weapons, but it was hoped that should the United States be able to relieve certain British vessels in other

U. S. SECRET
BRITISH MOST SECRET

Areas, then further British ships might be made available for the ABDA Area.

DR. VAN MOOK expressed his gratitude to the Combined Chiefs of Staff for allowing him to have the opportunity of discussing the situation with them, and said that he hoped that the Dutch Military Authorities in Washington might be afforded further opportunities to discuss the problems in which they were vitally interested.

(At this point, Dr. Van Mook, R. Adm. Ranneft and Colonel Weijerman left the meeting.)

9. MUNITIONS ASSIGNMENTS BOARD.
   (C.C.S. 19)

THE COMMITTEE had before them C.C.S. 19, containing an Order establishing the Munitions Assignments Board.

THE COMMITTEE:-

Instructed the Secretaries to circulate this Order* as amended in the course of discussion.

*Subsequently circulated as C.C.S. 19/1.

10. MOVE OF U.S. TROOPS TO NORTH IRELAND.
    (C.C.S. 11/1)

ADMIRAL LITTLE explained that Sir Dudley Pound, in answer to an inquiry from himself, had explained that only long-legged destroyers were suitable for the escort, and all those available in the Western Approaches were being used with WS convoys. In view of the fact that the TIRPITZ was at Trondjem, and German vessels might break out at Brest, Sir Dudley Pound was unwilling to immobilize the Home Fleet by diverting any destroyers from it. He was not clear as to the meaning of paragraph 1 of the Note, as the delay in the arrival of U.S. troops in Ireland was by no means "willingly" accepted by the British.

U. S. SECRET
BRITISH MOST SECRET

GENERAL MARSHALL said that he was in some doubt as to whether the Combined Chiefs of Staff were authorized to incur this additional delay to the combat-loaded ships required for GYMNAST.

SIR JOHN DILL explained that, as he saw it, GYMNAST would not be delayed, but rather that the period during which the necessary ships would be unavailable would be moved forward by nine days. He felt that the Combined Chiefs of Staff should accept the responsibility for this alteration, and that the combat-loaded ships should be used to convey U.S. troops to North Ireland on the later date necessitated by the fact that no escorts were available before then.

THE COMMITTEE:-

(a) Agreed that the U.S. combat-loaded ships should be used for the transfer of troops to Northern Ireland on the new date.

(b) Agreed to inform the President and the Prime Minister of the change of date, and of the effect on GYMNAST.

11. COOPERATION WITH GENERALISSIMO CHIANG KAI-SHEK.
(C.C.S. 22)

SIR JOHN DILL presented a draft telegram to General Wavell, informing him of Generalissimo Chiang Kai-Shek's views as set out in the enclosure to C.C.S. 22.

THE COMMITTEE:-

Instructed the Secretaries to despatch the draft telegram on receipt of the concurrence of the British Chiefs of Staff in London to its contents.

U. S. SECRET
BRITISH MOST SECRET

12. NAVAL ACTION IN THE PACIFIC

ADMIRAL LITTLE reminded the Committee that both the United States and British Chiefs of Staff in London had expressed their concern at the strategical situation now developing in the ABDA Area in almost identical terms. It was essential to halt the Japanese advance. The recent U.S. naval action in the Japanese mandates would have a most useful effect, and further action on the Japanese flank was the surest way of diverting the Japanese from their almost unmolested move to the South.

ADMIRAL KING said that as soon as possible he proposed to undertake further Naval action in the Japanese mandated area.

THE COMMITTEE:

Took note of the above statements.

13. INSTITUTION OF THE ANZAC AREA.
    (C.C.S. 15 and D.B.A. 7)

THE COMMITTEE:-

Took note that D.B.A. 7 had been despatched to General Wavell.

14. EMPLOYMENT OF A.V.G. IN BURMA AND CHINA.
    (C.C.S. 20)

THE COMMITTEE:-

Took note of this paper.

15. PORTUGUESE TIMOR.
    (C.C.S. 16 and D.B.A. 6)

SIR JOHN DILL and ADMIRAL LITTLE felt that the present threat to Timor was such that under the terms of the agreement with the Portu-

U. S. SECRET
BRITISH MOST SECRET

guese, it would be unnecessary to withdraw the Australian and Dutch forces.

THE COMMITTEE:-

Took note that D.B.A. 6 had been despatched to General Wavell.

16. COMMUNICATIONS BETWEEN GENERAL WAVELL AND GENERALISSIMO CHIANG KAI-SHEK.
(Previous reference: U.S. ABC4/9, British W.W. 10, paragraph-4d)

In reply to a question by Sir John Dill, GENERAL MARSHALL said that there would be no objection to General Wavell communicating direct with Generalissimo Chiang Kai-Shek, using existing wireless communications through the British Military Attache at Chungking, the Senior U.S. Liaison Officer with the Generalissimo being kept informed.

THE COMMITTEE:-

Took note of the above statement.

U. S. SECRET
BRITISH MOST SECRET

C.C.S. 4th Meeting.

COMBINED CHIEFS OF STAFF

MINUTES of a Meeting held in Room 340,
Public Health Building, on Tuesday, February
10, 1942, at 3:00 p.m.

PRESENT

Admiral H. R. Stark, USN	Field Marshal Sir John Dill
General G. C. Marshall, USA	Admiral Sir Charles Little
Admiral E. J. King, USN	Lt. General Sir Colville Wemyss
Lt. General H. H. Arnold, USA	Air Marshal D. C. S. Evill

THE FOLLOWING WERE ALSO PRESENT

Rear Admiral J.H. Towers, USN	Captain G. D. Belben, RN
Rear Admiral R.K. Turner, USN	Captain J. A. Grindle, RN
Brig. General L.T. Gerow, USA	Group Captain S. C. Strafford
Captain F.C. Denebrink, USN	Lt. Col. G. K. Bourne
Commander R.E. Libby, USN	
Lt. Col. E.L. Sibert, USA	

SECRETARIAT

Brigadier V. Dykes
Brig. Gen. W.B. Smith, USA
Commander L.R. McDowell, USN
Commander R.D. Coleridge, RN

U. S. SECRET
BRITISH MOST SECRET

1. ACCOMMODATION IN PUBLIC HEALTH BUILDING FOR JOINT STAFF MISSION.

SIR JOHN DILL expressed the appreciation of himself and the Heads of the Joint Staff Mission for the generous offer of accommodation in the Public Health Building made by the Joint U.S. Chiefs of Staff-- an offer which the Joint Staff Mission most gratefully accepted.

2. APPOINTMENTS OF BRITISH FLAG OFFICERS.

ADMIRAL LITTLE stated that Admiral Somerville would be leaving the United Kingdom on about February 15, 1942, in H.M.S. FORMIDABLE to assume command of the Eastern Fleet, with his Headquarters in Ceylon. Admiral Tennant was proceeding in H.M.S. NEWCASTLE to assume command of the British Naval forces in the ABDA Area.

THE COMMITTEE:-

Took note of the above statements.

3. WAR COLLABORATION BETWEEN UNITED NATIONS.
(Previous reference: C.C.S. 1st Meeting, Minute 9, C.C.S.9)

The Representatives of the British Chiefs of Staff presented certain amendments to C.C.S. 9.

After discussion, *THE COMMITTEE:-*

Approved C.C.S. 9, as amended in the course of discussion, and instructed the Secretariat to issue the amended version.*

*Subsequently circulated as C.C.S. 9/1

4. COMBINED INTELLIGENCE.
(C.C.S. 23)

U. S. SECRET
BRITISH MOST SECRET

THE COMMITTEE:-

Accepted this Paper.

5. COMBINED MILITARY TRANSPORTATION COMMITTEE.
(C.C.S. 24)

The Representatives of the British Chiefs of Staff presented certain minor amendments to this Paper.

THE COMMITTEE:-

Accepted C.C.S. 24, as amended in the course of discussion, and instructed the Secretariat to issue the amended version of this Paper, in form of a Directive.*

*Subsequently circulated as C.C.S. 24/1.

6. THE ECONOMICAL EMPLOYMENT OF AIR FORCES AGAINST JAPAN.
(C.C.S. 34)

THE COMMITTEE:-

Agreed to refer the paper to the Combined Staff Planners for examination, as a basis for a comprehensive review of the strategical situation in the Japanese Theater of War (including the entire Pacific area) and the preparation of a combined plan for the forces of the United Nations in the area, including:-

   (a) The roles to be played by the Eastern and Pacific fleets, the broad distribution of naval forces and the naval bases which must consequently be held and developed.

   (b) The air forces required to defend essential naval and air bases, for the control of sea areas, and for

U. S. SECRET
BRITISH MOST SECRET

        building up the air offensive.

    (c)   The land forces required to hold base areas in the first defensive stage and the organization of amphibious striking forces for the assumption of the offensive.

This plan would lead up to the determination of the total forces required and the manner of their provision.

7.   AIR REQUIREMENTS FOR AUSTRALIA AND NEW ZEALAND.
    (Previous Reference: C.C.S. 3rd Meeting, Minute 7, C.C.S. 30)

AIR MARSHAL EVILL explained that the estimated requirements for Australia and New Zealand had altered somewhat since the paper under discussion had been drafted. The Australian requirement was now considered to be 250 pursuit aircraft, whereas New Zealand was asking for four fighter squadrons as formed units.

GENERAL ARNOLD presented a memorandum by the U.S. Chiefs of Staff.* He said that the United States production of pursuit planes was now at its lowest ebb, but from now on would increase. He felt that a complete study of the aircraft production of the United Nations, to include medium and heavy bombers as well as pursuit planes, should be undertaken at once; and that only with this review before them could the Combined Chiefs of Staff deal with the whole problem of the allocation of our production.

    *Subsequently circulated as C.C.S. 30/1.

AIR MARSHAL EVILL said that the diversion of the P-40's set out in paragraph 2 of C.C.S. 30 from British resources would go forward.

    THE COMMITTEE:-

    (a)   Instructed the Combined Staff Planners, in collab-

U. S. SECRET
BRITISH MOST SECRET

oration with the Munitions Assignments Board, to prepare a review of the aircraft production of the United Nations and the requirements of the various theaters of war as early as possible.

(b) Took note that pending the completion of this review, the United States could not immediately allocate any pursuit aircraft to Australia and New Zealand, except possibly at the expense of pursuit squadrons now set up for "MAGNET," a suggestion which the British Chiefs of Staff would examine.

8. ADDITIONAL FIGHTER TYPE AIRCRAFT TO THE NETHERLANDS EAST INDIES.
(C.C.S. 33)

ADMIRAL KING pointed out that in this case the Munitions Assignments Board appeared to be initiating action, instead of following a Directive by the Combined Chiefs of Staff.

GENERAL MARSHALL said he understood that the Munitions Assignments Board had given a provisional promise to the Dutch authorities that at least the original 36 of these aircraft would be forthcoming. If this were so, any reversal of this promise, however informal, would cause considerable embarrassment. The Munitions Assignments Board were under constant fire from the Russians, and resulting from the Rio de Janeiro Conference, many other demands, particularly for aircraft and spare parts, had been made by the South American nations taking part in it. As far as shipping the aircraft was concerned, the Dutch authorities in Washington had informed him that they had available space in Dutch ships.

It was suggested that the Combined Chiefs of Staff should approve the allocation of the first 36 P-40 fighters, but that they should be allocated to the ABDA Area, and not specifically to the Dutch.

ADMIRAL TOWERS however, pointed out the difficulties in this

U. S. SECRET
BRITISH MOST SECRET

procedure, particularly with regard to certain special equipment which would have to be fitted to the aircraft before they left this country if they were to be used by Dutch personnel.

    THE COMMITTEE:-

        (a) Approved the despatch of the first 36 P-40 fighters to the ABDA Area for the use of the Dutch--these aircraft to be transported in Dutch bottoms.

        (b) Agreed to reconsider the question of the second 36 P-40 aircraft in two weeks' time.

9.   SITUATION IN THE NETHERLANDS EAST INDIES.
      (C.C.S. 31)

ADMIRAL KING explained that the enclosure to C.C.S. 31 contained a translation of a despatch from the Commander in Chief of the Netherlands East Indies Fleet (Admiral Helfrich) to the Secretary of the Dutch Navy in London. The Dutch Naval Attache had given him (Admiral King) a copy of this despatch.

Both ADMIRAL STARK and ADMIRAL KING were of the opinion that the views expressed in the latter part of Admiral Helfrich's despatch should more properly have been referred by him in the first instance to General Wavell.

    THE COMMITTEE:-

    Invited Admiral King, on behalf of the Combined Chiefs of Staff, to ask the Dutch Naval Attache to find out whether Admiral Helfrich had represented these views to General Wavell.

10.   NAVAL COMMAND IN THE ABDA AREA.
      (C.C.S. 32)

U. S. SECRET
BRITISH MOST SECRET

THE COMMITTEE were informed that the announcement of the designation of Vice Admiral Helfrich as Acting Commander of the Combined Naval Forces in the ABDA Area would be released at 2 p.m. G.C.T. on the following day, Wednesday, February 11, 1942.

ADMIRAL KING stated that Admiral Hart would return home and make his report in his status as Commander in Chief, U.S. Asiatic Fleet.

THE COMMITTEE:-

Took note of the above statements.

11. PROPOSAL FOR BLOCKING TORRES STRAIT WITH MINES.
    (C.C.S. 36)

ADMIRAL STARK stated that the word "main" should be inserted before the words "Naval base" in line 5 of paragraph 2 of this paper.

It was felt that General Wavell's concurrence to the proposal to block the Torres Strait should be sought prior to a decision being given.

THE COMMITTEE:-

(a) Instructed the Secretaries to despatch the draft telegram* contained in C.C.S. 36 to General Wavell, as amended in the course of discussion.

(b) Took note that Admiral King would despatch the draft telegram** contained in C.C.S. 36 to Admiral Leary, as amended in the course of discussion.

* Subsequently despatched as D.B.A./4.

**Subsequently despatched as Cominch's 102115 to COMANZAC Force.

U. S. SECRET
BRITISH MOST SECRET

12. CHANGE IN WESTERN ATLANTIC AREA AS DEFINED IN ABC-1.
    (C.C.S. 1/1)

    THE COMMITTEE:-

    Took note that Admiral King and Admiral Little would give further consideration to these proposals.

13. PROPOSALS TO BOLSTER CHINESE MORALE.

    ADMIRAL STARK presented a memorandum prepared by the U.S. Special Study Group containing a proposal that both the President and the Prime Minister should send telegrams to Generalissimo Chiang Kai-Shek expressing their appreciation of the importance of the role which had been, and was being played by the Chinese armies and peoples under his leadership.

    THE COMMITTEE:-

    (a) Expressed the opinion that any action designed to improve Chinese morale was militarily desirable. Approved in principle the proposals contained in the memorandum.

    (b) Agreed that the U.S. Chiefs of Staff should submit the proposal to the President and that the Representatives of the British Chiefs of Staff should take parallel action with respect to the Prime Minister.

14. TELEGRAM TO GENERAL WAVELL EXPRESSING THE APPRECIATION OF THE COMBINED CHIEFS OF STAFF.

    GENERAL MARSHALL suggested that the Combined Chiefs of Staff should send a telegram to General Wavell, expressing their appreciation of his handling of the difficult situation in the ABDA Area.

U. S. SECRET
BRITISH MOST SECRET

GENERAL MARSHALL then presented a draft telegram.

THE COMMITTEE:-

(a) Expressed their approval of the terms of the telegram as drafted by General Marshall.

(b) Took note that the draft telegram would be referred to the British Chiefs of Staff in London for their approval prior to its despatch.

15. SECRECY OF GENERAL WAVELL'S A.W. TELEGRAMS.

SIR JOHN DILL said that he had received a personal message from General Wavell, requesting that particular care should be taken to ensure that his A.W. series of telegrams was given only a very limited circulation, and handled with particular care from the point of view of secrecy.

THE COMMITTEE:-

Took note of the above statement.

U. S. SECRET
BRITISH MOST SECRET

C.C.S. 5th Meeting.

COMBINED CHIEFS OF STAFF

MINUTES of a Meeting held in Room 340, Public Health Building, on Tuesday, February 17, 1942, at 3:00 p.m.

PRESENT

Admiral H. R. Stark, USN	Field Marshal Sir John Dill
General G. C. Marshall, USA	Admiral Sir Charles Little
Admiral E. J. King, USN	Lt. General Sir Colville Wemyss
Lt. General H.H. Arnold, USA	Air Marshal D. C. S. Evill

THE FOLLOWING WERE ALSO PRESENT

Rear Admiral J. H. Towers, USN	Captain G. D. Belben, RN
Rear Admiral R. K. Turner, USN	Group Captain S.C. Strafford
Captain F. C. Denebrink, USN	
Colonel T. T. Handy, USA	
Commander R. E. Libby, USN	
Lt. Col. E. L. Sibert, USN	
Major J. C. Holmes, USA	

SECRETARIAT

Brigadier V. Dykes
Brig. Gen. W. B. Smith, USA
Commander L.R. McDowell, USN
Commander R.D. Coleridge, RN

U. S. SECRET
BRITISH MOST SECRET

1. THE GENERAL SITUATION IN THE ABDA AND ANZAC AREAS.
   (ABDACOM Signals C.C.O.S. 4, 7 and 8)

SIR JOHN DILL drew attention to a personal telegram* from General Wavell to the Prime Minister and himself, copies of which had been sent to the U.S. Chiefs of Staff.

He said that he felt that from a purely military point of view, General Wavell's recommendation that at least the first Division of the Australian Corps should be sent to Burma was the correct one. To accept the fact that no further reinforcements should be put into Java was a hard decision to take, but he felt sure it was the right one. The ultimate defeat of Japan depended upon the United Nations holding Burma and Australia. There might be a strong political pull from Australia to divert the whole of the Australian Corps to Australia, rather than to Burma. The political aspect would have to be considered in London. The disposal of the second Australian Division could be considered at a later date, as it was not due in the Area for from three to four weeks.

SIR JOHN DILL emphasized the importance of having good fighting troops in Burma, in view of the doubtful value of the Burmese troops.

ADMIRAL STARK stated that the U.S. Chiefs of Staff had come to the same conclusion, i.e., that the reinforcement of Java was not a sound military proposition.

SIR JOHN DILL then raised the question of Burma reverting to the India Command. With the loss of Java, the ABDA Area would be cut in half, and the control of Burma could be more effectively exercised from India.

Sir John Dill then presented a draft telegram. He felt that at some later date the boundaries of the ABDA Area might have to be reconsidered, but that the elimination of Burma from the ABDA Command should be dealt with first.

*ABDACOM 01288 of 16/2.

U. S. SECRET
BRITISH MOST SECRET

ADMIRAL KING stated that the Northern ANZAC Area was vital to the maintenance of our position in Australia. The center of gravity of the U.S. Pacific Fleet was moving to the southward. It was essential to get an articulated series of strong points between Hawaii and Australia. Units of the U.S. Pacific Fleet, together with ANZAC Naval forces, were now operating in this area. It might be necessary to consider whether it were not desirable that the ANZAC Area should be regarded as a U.S. sphere of activity, in that the operations therein were closely related to those of the U.S. Pacific Fleet. The Burma, India, and China spheres on the other hand, could only be regarded as primarily British.

GENERAL MARSHALL said that with regard to the Eastern ABDA Area, we had now reached the point where strong naval operations in the waters northeast of Australia might have to be undertaken with light air support; whereas it had previously been envisaged that the naval forces would not be strong, and that the operations would be undertaken mainly by air forces.

AIR MARSHAL EVILL said that he felt it was essential to consolidate our base for an offensive. Bases in eastern Australia were relatively adequate, but in northern Australia the bases would have to be built up, and Darwin might have to be covered from bases well in the rear. Naval operations without strong air support were, he felt, a most unwise undertaking. The enemy fully appreciated this point, and his air bases had advanced step by step in conformity with the areas used for his naval operations. We were now at a stage where we must build up a strong force with adequate bases, and then pass to a combined and interdependent air and naval offensive. We had previously made the mistake of moving air forces too far forward, and operating them from inadequately protected bases.

ADMIRAL STARK drew attention to General Wavell's request contained in C.C.O.S. 4 for an appreciation from the Combined Chiefs of Staff on their views on the strategy to be adopted vis-a-vis Japan.

U. S. SECRET
BRITISH MOST SECRET

THE COMMITTEE:-

(a) Instructed the Secretaries to despatch the draft telegram* to General Wavell, as amended in the course of discussion.

(b) Agreed that on the facts as presented by General Wavell, it appeared militarily unsound to reinforce Java, and that at least the first Australian Division should be diverted to Burma; but that in view of the political considerations involved, no final decisions could be taken until the recommendations of the Pacific Council in London were available.

(c) Took note that the Combined Staff Planners were preparing an appreciation of the Japanese situation, which, when approved by the Combined Chiefs of Staff could be sent to General Wavell in reply to his telegram No. C.C.O.S. 4.

*Subsequently despatched as D.B.A. 17.

2. RELATION OF MERCHANT SHIPPING LOSSES TO THE PROSECUTION OF THE WAR.
(C.C.S. 39)

SIR JOHN DILL said that though the subject of shipping was being discussed at a meeting of the Munitions Assignments Board on the following day, at which Sir Arthur Salter would be present, he felt it important that the Combined Chiefs of Staff should give preliminary consideration to the very important implications of the present shipping situation brought to light in C.C.S. 39.

SIR JOHN DILL added that the representatives of the British Chiefs of Staff had also received a telegram on the shipping position from the Chiefs of Staff in London pointing out that we should be unable to provide amply to meet the full scale of attack in both the Middle

U. S. SECRET
BRITISH MOST SECRET

East and Far East, and might well be faced with the great problem of deciding between them. A strong committee, under the Minister of War Transport, was now investigating the problem, and it was most unlikely that any remedies, including the most drastic inroads in the British import program, could bridge the gap between requirements and capacity. The representatives of the British Chiefs of Staff were invited to bring this position to the notice of the U.S. Chiefs of Staff, and to emphasize that unless it was found possible to produce more shipping, particularly personnel shipping from United States sources, we might shortly be faced with the choice of risking either the Middle East or Far East.

SIR JOHN DILL said that he felt that possibly the losses for 1942 might have been slightly over estimated in view of the fact that the early part of the year had previously proved to be that part in which the most serious losses were experienced.

ADMIRAL KING said that some alleviation might be afforded by the new plan whereby convoys would use the Great Circle Route rather than going farther northward near Greenland where heavy winter gales were experienced.

GENERAL MARSHALL said that he was planning to ship a further 23,000 men to the ABDA Area, and it was hoped to find sufficient shipping to permit them to sail in the first week in March. He was, however, seriously worried on the limitations imposed on the war effort of the United Nations by the shipping position, and he read extracts from a note from himself to Admiral Land pointing out that though $1\frac{1}{2}$ million U.S. troops would be ready for service overseas by the end of 1942 and $3\frac{1}{2}$ million by the end of 1943, it appeared that less than half of these troops could, in fact, be shipped and maintained in an overseas theater of war. He felt that the whole subject should, in the first instance, be examined by the Combined Military Transportation Committee in consultation with the Combined Staff Planners in order that the Chiefs of Staff should have before them a picture of the implications of the shipping position on strategical possibilities, including the undertaking of such Operations as "GYMNAST."

U. S. SECRET
BRITISH MOST SECRET

THE COMMITTEE:-

Instructed the Combined Military Transportation Committee, in collaboration with the Combined Staff Planners to examine the memorandum (C.C.S. 39), and to furnish a report to the Combined Chiefs of Staff on its implications in respect to:-

(a) The reinforcement and maintenance of the European, Middle East and Far East theaters.

(b) The possibility of undertaking Operation "GYMNAST."

3. PRIORITIES DIRECTIVE.

GENERAL MARSHALL drew the attention of the Committee to the shortage of certain essential raw materials which was holding up the manufacture of weapons. Certain alleviation was being obtained through the cessation of commercial production, but this was relatively small, and it was essential that some simple guide, based on our strategic policy, should be given to the authorities responsible for production.

THE COMMITTEE:-

Instructed the Combined Staff Planners to consult with the Munitions Assignments Board as to the best method of arriving at a broad directive on a strategical basis for the general priorities in the production of the critical weapons of war, such as aircraft, tanks, combat and other ships, A.A., artillery etc. The purpose of this directive would be to obtain from the Munitions Assignments Board a "trial balance sheet" for materiel on which the priorities to be accorded to critical items could be more precisely determined by the Combined Chiefs of Staff.

4. NAVAL, ARMY AND AIR FORCES IN THE ABDA AND ANZAC AREAS.
(C.C.S. 41)

U. S. SECRET
BRITISH MOST SECRET

SIR JOHN DILL said that he thought the Japanese claim of 60,000 prisoners in Singapore was substantially correct. This would include 10,000 Australians and at least 15,000 British troops.

THE COMMITTEE:-

Took note of this paper.

5. NAVAL REINFORCEMENTS FOR THE ABDA AREA.
(Previous Reference: C.C.S. 3rd Meeting, Minute 3, C.C.S. 2/2)

ADMIRAL KING said that this suggestion, that further reinforcements should be sent to the ABDA Area, would be covered in the appreciation being produced by the Combined Staff Planners. He had been distressed to learn that the U.S. cruiser "PHOENIX," which had been sent to the ABDA Area to relieve the "BOISE," had been delayed for some two weeks in Melbourne in spite of his instructions allocating her to the ABDA Area. She was, however, now on her way to Freemantle.

THE COMMITTEE:-

Took note of the paper.

6. TORRES STRAITS.
(Previous Reference: C.C.S. 4th Meeting, Minute 11)

ADMIRAL KING said that as yet no reply to D.B.A. 14 had been received from General Wavell. COMANZAC had, however, given his views.

ADMIRAL KING then read out a telegram from Admiral Leary which suggested that in view of the navigational difficulties in the Torres Straits, and the possibility that the enemy could sweep a channel should mines be laid, he did not recommend for the present laying mines in this area.

ADMIRAL LITTLE said that the Admiralty had given him their views which were in general similar to those of Admiral Leary. Owing to

- 48 -

U. S. SECRET
BRITISH MOST SECRET

the strength of the tidal streams in various channels, it was not practicable to use either moored or magnetic mines in the channels themselves. To cover the approaches of the various channels would require more mines than were available from British sources; should the enemy sweep a channel, we should be at a disadvantage as the enemy would know the swept channel and we should not; should the Japanese gain control of either the southern shore of New Guinea or of the York Peninsula, the minefield would be of no value.

ADMIRAL KING reminded the Committee that the proposal had in the first instance been made in December by the Australians. He was prepared to accept the views of the local commanders, and to drop the proposal for the present.

THE COMMITTEE:-

Agreed that unless General Wavell advocated the blocking of the channel, the proposal should, for the present, be dropped.

7. DEFENSE OF WEST AFRICAN AIR ROUTE.
(C.C.S. 28)

SIR JOHN DILL said that the British Chiefs of Staff agreed with the recommendations contained in paragraph 6 of this paper, and asked if there were any way in which the British could be of assistance.

THE COMMITTEE:-

Agreed to accept the recommendations contained in paragraph 6 of C.C.S. 28.

8. TANK PRODUCTION OF THE UNITED NATIONS AND THE REQUIREMENTS OF VARIOUS THEATERS OF WAR.
(C.C.S. 35)

Both GENERAL MARSHALL and SIR JOHN DILL felt that it was unwise to deal with certain weapons individually, and that the directive

U. S. SECRET
BRITISH MOST SECRET

being prepared for the Munitions Assignments Board (vide Item 3) would cover the production and allocation of tanks.

THE COMMITTEE:-

Agreed with the views expressed above and instructed the Secretaries to so inform the Munitions Assignments Board.

9. ARRANGEMENTS FOR THE MOVEMENT OF TWO HEAVY BOMBARDMENT GROUPS OF THE U.S. ARMY AIR FORCES TO THE UNITED KINGDOM.
(C.C.S. 40)

GENERAL ARNOLD explained that it would be necessary to study further the proposal to send two U.S. Army pursuit groups to the United Kingdom.

AIR MARSHAL EVILL undertook to obtain the views of the British Air Staff on this point.

ADMIRAL KING stressed the difficulty of allocating the necessary shipping for the movement of the heavy bombardment groups so far ahead.

GENERAL ARNOLD explained that such a decision at the present stage was desirable in view of the necessary arrangements which would have to be made for the reception of the two groups in the United Kingdom.

AIR MARSHAL EVILL said that the arrangements for the reception of the two Heavy Bombardment Groups in the United Kingdom would, in any case, be made.

THE COMMITTEE agreed:-

  (a) That arrangements should proceed on the basis that the necessary shipping would be available to transport the two heavy bombardment groups to the United

U. S. SECRET
BRITISH MOST SECRET

               Kingdom in May.

       (b)   That it might at a later date be necessary to reconsider their destination.

10.   PROPOSAL TO BOLSTER CHINESE MORALE.
       (C.C.S. 38)

THE COMMITTEE:-

Took note of this paper.

U. S. SECRET
BRITISH MOST SECRET

C.C.S. 6th Meeting.

COMBINED CHIEFS OF STAFF

MINUTES of a Meeting held in Room 340, Public Health Building, on Wednesday, February 18, 1942, at 12:30 p.m.

PRESENT

Admiral H. R. Stark, USN
General G. C. Marshall, USA
Admiral E. J. King, USN
Lt. General H.H. Arnold, USA

Field Marshal Sir John Dill
Admiral Sir Charles Little
Lt. General Sir Colville Wemyss
Air Marshal D. C. S. Evill

THE FOLLOWING WERE ALSO PRESENT

Rear Admiral J.H. Towers, USN
Rear Admiral R.K. Turner, USN
Captain F.C..Denebrink, USN
Colonel T. T. Handy, USA
Commander R. E. Libby, USN
Lt. Col. E. L. Sibert, USA
Major J. C. Holmes, USA

Captain J. A. Grindle, RN
Lt. Colonel G. K. Bourne

For Part of the Meeting:
R. Adm. J.E.M. Ranneft, RNN
 Dutch Naval Attache
Comdr. C.W.M. Vereker, RNZN
 New Zealand Naval Attache
Col. F.G.L. Weijerman, RNIA
 Dutch Military Attache

SECRETARIAT

Brigadier V. Dykes
Brig. Gen. W.B. Smith, USA
Commander L.R. McDowell, USN
Commander R.D. Coleridge, RN

U. S. SECRET
BRITISH MOST SECRET

1. SITUATION IN THE ABDA AREA.
   (C.O.S. No. (W) 58)

   THE COMMITTEE had before them C.O.S. No. (W) 58, a telegram from the British Chiefs of Staff in London to the Combined Chiefs of Staff containing the resolutions agreed at a meeting of the Pacific War Council in London. In the course of discussion the following points were made:-

   (a) The telegram under consideration had been repeated to ABDACOM. Sir John Dill had sent a most immediate telegram to London suggesting that this should be cancelled.

   (b) Some concern was expressed that the Pacific War Council appeared to be usurping the functions of the Combined Chiefs of Staff in that they were exercising control over military strategy.

   (c) U.S. naval and air forces, including aircraft carriers, together with Australian vessels and aircraft, were already committed to operations immediately to the eastward of New Guinea which had as part of their object a diversionary effect on Japanese operations. Ten additional U.S. small submarines were being diverted to the southwest Pacific in April.

   (d) GENERAL MARSHALL had received a despatch from General Brett announcing his intention to divert to the Burma area equipment and ground personnel required for two heavy bomber squadrons now on the way to the ABDA Area from the westward, some of which were already at Rangoon and others en route. He also proposed that the personnel and equipment of three pursuit squadrons should be similarly diverted to the Burma area though it was not clear if this included the aircraft themselves.

U. S. SECRET
BRITISH MOST SECRET

    (e) In connection with (d) above, AIR MARSHAL EVILL pointed out that this appeared to be in pursuance of a previous suggestion from General Brett to transfer air forces from Australia to Burma. While Burma remained within his command such a small diversion was within the rights of ABDACOM but as a matter of policy it appeared sounder that in general air forces operating from Burma should be supplied and maintained from the United Kingdom or Middle East, whereas those in Australia should be supplied and maintained from the United States. He would, however, refer the matter to the Air Staff in London for their views.

    (f) The Committee was reminded of the United States' obligation to assist the Chinese and of the strategic concept of finally bombing Japan from bases in Free China.

THE COMMITTEE then considered a draft telegram from the Combined Chiefs of Staff to ABDACOM based on C.O.S. No. (W) 58, and certain amendments were made to this draft.

(At this point R. Adm. Ranneft, Dutch Naval Attache, Colonel Weijerman, Dutch Military Attache, and Commander Vereker, New Zealand Naval Attache, entered the meeting.)

After considering the draft telegram as amended, COLONEL WEIJERMAN explained that the forces now in Java were insufficient to hold the island against a determined attack. They consisted only of four combat teams, each of one regiment, together with some artillery. The total forces of all kinds in the island amounted to 60,000 but of these less than 40,000 were combat troops. The Dutch Commander in Chief had some three weeks ago asked for further reinforcements but he realized that due to the time factor and the shipping difficulties it had not been possible to make these available.

U. S. SECRET
BRITISH MOST SECRET

R. Adm. Ranneft, Colonel Weijerman and Commander Vereker then gave their concurrence to the telegram to ABDACOM.

THE COMMITTEE:-

Agreed that the draft telegram as amended should be submitted simultaneously to the President and the Prime Minister for their concurrence prior to its despatch as from the Combined Chiefs of Staff.

U. S. SECRET
BRITISH MOST SECRET

C.C.S. 7th Meeting.

COMBINED CHIEFS OF STAFF

MINUTES of a Meeting held in Room 240,
Public Health Building, on Saturday, February
21, 1942, at 3:00 p.m.

PRESENT

Admiral H. R. Stark, USN
General G. C. Marshall, USA
Admiral E. J. King, USN
Lt. General H.H. Arnold, USA

Field Marshal Sir John Dill
Admiral Sir Charles Little
Lt. General Sir Colville Wemyss
Air Marshal D. C. S. Evill

THE FOLLOWING WERE ALSO PRESENT

Rear Admiral J.H. Towers, USN
Rear Admiral R.K. Turner, USN
Captain Oscar Smith, USN
Captain F. C. Denebrink, USN
Colonel T. T. Handy, USA
Commander R. E. Libby, USN
Lt. Col. H. B. Hansell, USA
Lt. Col. E. L. Sibert, USA
Major J. C. Holmes, USA

The Rt. Hon. R. G. Casey
  (for part of the time)
Captain J. A. Grindle, RN

For Items 1&2:

R. Adm. J.E.M. Ranneft, RNN,
  Dutch Naval Attache

Maj. Gen. A.Q.H. Dyxhoorn, RNA
  Representative C.O.S.C.

Col. F.G.L. Weijerman, RNIA
  Dutch Military Attache

Commander D. H. Harries, RAN
  Australian Naval Attache

SECRETARIAT

Brigadier V. Dykes
Brig. Gen. W.B. Smith, USA
Commander L.R. McDowell, USN
Commander R.D. Coleridge, RN

U. S. SECRET
BRITISH MOST SECRET

1. SITUATION IN THE ABDA AREA.
   (ABDACOM Signal C.C.O.S. 16 and C.O.S. (W) 69)

THE COMMITTEE had before them ABDACOM Telegram C.C.O.S. 16 to the Combined Chiefs of Staff, and a Telegram from the Chiefs of Staff, London, to the Joint Staff Mission No. (W) 69.

A draft telegram prepared by the Combined Secretariat was presented for consideration.

(At this point, MR. CASEY entered the meeting.)

With regard to the suggestion contained in paragraph 3 of the telegram from the Chiefs of Staff, London, No. (W) 69, that the headquarters of ABDACOM should be set up at Freemantle, MR. CASEY said that he could see no point in the selection of Freemantle as General Wavell's future headquarters. The Australian Chiefs of Staff, together with Admiral Leary, the U.S. Attaches, and the U.S. officers responsible for the organization of American supplies in Australia, were all situated at Melbourne, at which point also excellent communications existed.

Both ADMIRAL STARK and SIR JOHN DILL felt that there was no particular reason for suggesting Freemantle to General Wavell, and that the establishment of headquarters at Darwin would not be practicable.

(At this point, MR. CASEY left the meeting.)

THE COMMITTEE were informed that the Pacific War Council were to meet in London at 2030 hrs. B.S.T. that evening.

The Dutch and Australian Representatives signified their concurrence to the draft telegram as amended in discussion.

It was agreed that the paragraph in the draft telegram dealing with policy with regard to evacuation of air forces, air personnel for whom there were no aircraft, and such troops as could not contribute to the defense of Java, would have to be referred to the President and the

U. S. SECRET
BRITISH MOST SECRET

Prime Minister prior to its despatch.

    THE COMMITTEE:-

        (a) Agreed to despatch that part of the draft telegram* not dealing with the points mentioned immediately above, to General Wavell.

        (b) Agreed to refer the remainder of the telegram to the President and the Prime Minister prior to its despatch.

        * Subsequently despatched as D.B.A. 20.

(Subsequent to the meeting, it was learned that the President's approval had been obtained.

2.   EXCLUSION OF BURMA FROM THE ABDA AREA.
     (D.B.A. 17 and ABDACOM Signal C.C.O.S. 14)

    THE COMMITTEE had before them D.B.A. 17 from the Combined Chiefs of Staff to ABDACOM, and C.C.O.S. 14 from ABDACOM to the Combined Chiefs of Staff.

    THE COMMITTEE considered a draft telegram to General Wavell, instructing him that Burma would revert to the operational command of India forthwith, and outlining the new provisional western boundary of the ABDA Area.

    THE COMMITTEE:-

Instructed the Secretaries to despatch this telegram*, as amended in the course of discussion, to General Wavell.

* Subsequently despatched as D.B.A. 21.

U. S. SECRET
BRITISH MOST SECRET

3.   COMMAND IN NEW CALEDONIA.

SIR JOHN DILL said that one of the Free French representatives had visited him to discuss the question of command in New Caledonia.

ADMIRAL D'ARGENLIEU had heard from the U.S. Liaison Officer there, of the intention to send an American force to the island and wished to be assured that he would be in command. The Free French representative had been told that this would not be a practicable proposition, but that the Admiral would have to be treated on the same basis vis-a-vis the United States forces as were the British Governors in the islands containing leased bases.

SIR JOHN DILL said he would circulate the terms of the message which the Free French representative had been instructed to give him.

U. S. SECRET
BRITISH MOST SECRET

C. C. S. 8th Meeting

COMBINED CHIEFS OF STAFF

MINUTES of a Meeting held in Room 240,
Public Health Building, on Monday, February
23, 1942, at 3:00 p.m.

PRESENT

Admiral H. R. Stark, USN	Field Marshal Sir John Dill
General G. C. Marshall, USA	Admiral Sir Charles Little
Admiral E. J. King, USN	Lt. General Sir Colville Wemyss
Lt. General H.H. Arnold, USA	Air Marshal D. C. S. Evill

THE FOLLOWING WERE ALSO PRESENT

Rear Admiral J.H. Towers, USN	Captain G. D. Belben, RN
Rear Admiral R.K. Turner, USN	Air Commodore S. C. Strafford
Captain Oscar Smith, USN	For Part of Meeting:
Captain F. C. Denebrink, USN	Maj. Gen. A.Q.H. Dyxhoorn, RNA
Colonel T. T. Handy, USA	Representative C.O.S.C.
Commander R. E. Libby, USN	R. Adm. J.E.M. Ranneft, RNN
Lt. Col. E. L. Sibert, USA	Dutch Naval Attache
Major J. C. Holmes, USA	Commander D. H. Harries, RAN
Major R. L. Vittrup, USA	Australian Naval Attache
	Commander C.W.M. Vereker, RNZN
	New Zealand Naval Attache
	Col. F. G. L. Weijerman, RNIA
	Dutch Military Attache

SECRETARIAT

Brigadier V. Dykes
Brig. Gen. W.B. Smith, USA
Commander R. D. Coleridge, RN

U. S. SECRET
BRITISH MOST SECRET

1. SITUATION IN THE ABDA AREA.

THE COMMITTEE had before them ABDACOM Signals Nos. C.C.O.S. 19 and 20, and a telegram from the British Chiefs of Staff to the Joint Staff Mission No. (W) 76.

With regard to the suggestion contained in General Wavell's signal, and in the signal from the British Chiefs of Staff referred to above, that the ABDA Area as such should disappear, and that a line should be drawn, to the east of which the United States would exercise strategic control, and to the west of which the United Kingdom would exercise such control, GENERAL MARSHALL said that he was loath at this stage to see the ABDA organization, which had been so laboriously set up, being completely abolished.

ADMIRAL LITTLE explained that as he saw it the proposed line of demarkation was so designed that Naval forces could watch the passages of the Malay Barrier through which the Japanese forces could approach the Indian Ocean.

GENERAL MARSHALL then read out a personal despatch he had received from Lt. Governor Van Mook.

This despatch strongly deprecated the abandonment of the ABDA Command. Van Mook suggested that with adequate air support the position in Java could be held for at least several weeks. It was essential to get in fighters from the LANGLEY and the INDOMITABLE, and action by heavy bombers based outside Java was also necessary.

GENERAL MARSHALL pointed out that his despatch differed very considerably from the views expressed by the Governor of the Netherlands East Indies as reported by General Wavell.

THE COMMITTEE then considered a draft communique on the subject of the withdrawal of General Wavell, and a draft telegram to General Wavell in reply to his telegrams Nos. C.C.O.S. 19 and 20.

U. S. SECRET
BRITISH MOST SECRET

(At this point, GENERAL DYXHOORN, ADMIRAL RANNEFT, COLONEL WEIJERMAN, COMMANDER HARRIES and COMMANDER VEREKER entered the meeting.)

After a preliminary discussion on these drafts, GENERAL DYXHOORN asked whether a complete decision had been reached on the abolition of the ABDA Area, and if so, whether the reallocation of spheres of responsibility would be made before or after the fall of Java.

ADMIRAL STARK explained that no decision as to the splitting up of the ABDA Area was being taken at this time. The question was whether the Dutch were prepared to take over the command of the ABDA Area on the departure of General Wavell.

It was explained that certain British and Australian naval, land and air commanders would remain in Java, and that the flow of supplies already allocated to the ABDA Command would most certainly continue.

GENERAL DYXHOORN said that the Dutch would be prepared to accept command of the Area on General Wavell's departure. He had been informed from Java that the flow of supplies was being stopped, and had received an urgent request that fighters should be shipped from Australia.

GENERAL ARNOLD explained that the LANGLEY was not taking pursuit planes to Java.

ADMIRAL STARK then asked the Dutch and Dominion representatives to consider the possibility of the removal of northwest Australia from the ABDA Command. This step, if decided upon, would in no way stop the flow of supplies from Australia to the ABDA Area, or deprive that area of the air forces in northwest Australia now assigned to it.

After considering the draft communique and the draft telegram to General Wavell, the Dutch and Dominion representatives gave their assent to these two documents.

U. S. SECRET
BRITISH MOST SECRET

It was pointed out that these two documents had not yet received the approval of higher authority, more particularly as the British Government had not yet given its approval to the proposal that General Wavell should assume the post of Commander in Chief, India.

(At this point, GENERAL DYXHOORN, ADMIRAL RANNEFT, and COLONEL WEIJERMAN left the meeting.)

Further discussion then took place on the question of the removal of northern Australia from the ABDA Area, which would then be a Dutch Command.

It was pointed out that northwest Australia provided a valuable base from which long range bombers might operate over the ABDA Area, and the decision with regard to the responsibility of the defense of Darwin would be left in considerable doubt.

GENERAL MARSHALL pointed out the fact that the removal of northwest Australia from the ABDA Area simultaneously with its being turned over to the Dutch command, might have a very adverse effect on public opinion, as it might be construed as abandoning the Dutch in difficult circumstances.

THE COMMITTEE:-

(a) Agreed that consideration of the subdivision of the ABDA Area should for the present be deferred.

(b) Agreed that at present northwest Australia should remain within the ABDA Area.

(c) Instructed the Combined Staff Planners to recommend a line of demarkation between the Pacific and Indian Ocean predicated on the assumption that Java fell to the Japanese.

U. S. SECRET
BRITISH MOST SECRET

    (d) Agreed to despatch the two draft telegrams* to General Wavell, as amended in the course of discussion, on the receipt of the approval of the President, and of the Prime Minister on the passage relating to the resumption of command in India by General Wavell.

   *Subsequently despatched as D.B.A. Nos. 23 and 25.

2. PROPOSED TRANSFER OF TWO BRITISH SUBMARINES FROM THE ABDA AREA TO THE EASTERN FLEET.
  (C.C.S. 48)

  ADMIRAL STARK and ADMIRAL KING expressed agreement with the proposal contained in the above memorandum.

  ADMIRAL LITTLE then presented a draft telegram instructing General Wavell to release the two British submarines to the Eastern Fleet.

  THE COMMITTEE:-

    (a) Expressed their approval of the draft telegram.

    (b) Instructed the Secretaries to despatch it.*

   *Subsequently despatched as D.B.A. 24.

3. POLICY FOR DISPOSITION OF U.S. AND BRITISH AIR FORCES.
  (C.C.S. 47)

  SIR JOHN DILL pointed out that this paper contained only the bare outline of the situation and would require further study by the Combined Staff Planners.

  It was agreed that the two papers dealing with the Air Defense of Fiji and New Zealand (C.C.S. 45) and the Movement of two U.S. Pursuit Squadrons to Egypt (C.C.S. 46) should be included in the survey to

U. S. SECRET
BRITISH MOST SECRET

be made by the Combined Staff Planners.

GENERAL ARNOLD pointed out that the proposals contained in C.C.S. 47 visualized United States air forces operating in scattered units over the entire world, a policy to which he was opposed.

AIR MARSHAL EVILL explained that a telegram had been received from the British Chiefs of Staff in London elaborating the proposals. The building up of a bomber striking force in the U.K. will remain the fundamental policy, but the pressure of events in the Middle East and Far East had necessitated the suggestions for certain diversions. The main diversions were:

(a) The building up of a heavy bomber force in India.

(b) Additional heavy bomber forces in the Middle East. From the shipping aspect this commitment could more economically be undertaken by the United States rather than that the U.S. heavy bombers should be operated from the U.K., while the U.K. heavy bomber squadrons should move to the Middle East.

The whole proposal to send U.S. heavy bomber groups to the Middle East and Far East was limited to a total diversion of 4 groups.

With regard to pursuit planes, the two proposals by the British Chiefs of Staff were:

(a) That the U.S. should be asked to provide two pursuit groups for the Middle East, to make good the shortage resulting from the move of 9 British fighter squadrons from the Middle East to the Far East.

(b) That the U.S. should provide pursuit squadrons for Australia and New Zealand to secure the essential air and naval bases in these countries.

U. S. SECRET
BRITISH MOST SECRET

      ADMIRAL TURNER pointed out that the present directive to the Combined Staff Planners to prepare a review of strategic requirements for aircraft covered only the employment of forces against Japan, and suggested the terms of reference should be broadened to cover the requirements of all theaters.

      THE COMMITTEE:-

Instructed the Combined Staff Planners to consider C.C.S. 45, 46 and 47, together with C.C.S. 30 and 30/1, and to prepare, in collaboration with the Munitions Assignments Board, a review of the aircraft production of the United Nations, and the strategic requirements of the various theaters of war.

4.   COMMAND IN NEW CALEDONIA.
     (C.C.S. 44)

      SIR JOHN DILL said that he felt that there were two alternatives which might be adopted with regard to the suggestions contained in this document, either:

      (a)   ADMIRAL D'ARGENLIEU should continue in his capacity as Civil Governor in cooperation with the United States Commander of all the forces, as does the British Governor of a territory in which a U.S. leased base is situated.

      (b)   He could assume the command of the Free French forces in New Caledonia, subordinate to the United States Commander in the Islands.

      ADMIRAL KING pointed out that New Caledonia was only one of many Free French islands in the Pacific which could only be protected by United States forces. It was, therefore, essential to get the principle of command clearly defined.

U. S. SECRET
BRITISH MOST SECRET

THE COMMITTEE:-

Invited Sir John Dill to reply to M. Tixier on the lines he had suggested.

5. COMBINED METEOROLOGICAL COMMITTEE.
(C.C.S. 37)

GENERAL ARNOLD explained the importance of the adequate organization of a world-wide Meteorological Service properly coordinated and making better use of the information at our disposal, particularly long range weather prognostication.

THE COMMITTEE:-

(a) Accepted C.C.S. 37.

(b) Took note that the U.S. Chiefs of Staff would arrange for the participation of the Governments of the U.S.S.R., China and Netherlands, and that the Representatives of the British Chiefs of Staff would similarly arrange for the participation of the Dominions.

6. MADAGASCAR.
(C.C.S. 42 and 43)

SIR JOHN DILL explained that a plan for the occupation of Diego Suarez had been prepared, but that shortage of forces and more particularly of shipping made it doubtful as to how soon it could be put into effect.

ADMIRAL STARK felt that it was militarily most desirable to occupy Diego Suarez in order to deny this valuable base to the enemy, but that the decision to undertake such an operation could only be taken on political level, and after due consideration of the effects on our relations with Vichy.

U. S. SECRET
BRITISH MOST SECRET

    THE COMMITTEE:-

Agreed that while militarily the occupation of Diego Suarez was important, forces were not at present available, and the decision to undertake such an operation would be dependent on political considerations.

U. S. SECRET
BRITISH MOST SECRET

C.C.S. 9th Meeting.

COMBINED CHIEFS OF STAFF

MINUTES of meeting held in Room 240,
Public Health Building, on Tuesday, March
3, 1942, at 2:30 p.m.

PRESENT

Admiral H. R. Stark, USN	Field Marshal Sir John Dill
General G. C. Marshall, USA	Admiral Sir Charles Little
Admiral E. J. King, USN	Lt. General Sir Colville Wemyss
Lt. General H.H. Arnold, USA	Air Marshal D. C. S. Evill

THE FOLLOWING WERE ALSO PRESENT

Rear Admiral J.H. Towers, USN	Brigadier G. K. Bourne
Rear Admiral R.K. Turner, USN	Commander D. H. Harries, RAN
Captain Oscar Smith, USN	Australian Naval Attache
Captain F. C. Denebrink, USN	Commander C.W.M. Vereker, RNZN
Colonel T. T. Handy, USA	New Zealand Naval Attache
Commander R. E. Libby, USN	Captain J. A. Grindle, RN
Major J. C. Holmes, USA	

For Items 1 & 2:
  Maj. Gen. A.Q.H. Dyxhoorn, RNA
    Representative C.O.S.C.
  R. Adm. J. E. M. Ranneft, RNN
    Dutch Naval Attache
  Col. F. G. L. Weijerman, RNIA
    Dutch Military Attache

SECRETARIAT

Brigadier V. Dykes
Brig. Gen. W.B. Smith, USA
Commander L.R. McDowell, USN
Commander R.D. Coleridge, RN

U. S. SECRET
BRITISH MOST SECRET

1. SITUATION IN THE ABDA AREA.

GENERAL DYXHOORN gave an outline of the operations on and subsequent to February 27, 1942 in the ABDA Area. In reply to a question he said that the total number of Dutch troops in Java was 68,000 though not more than 40,000 of these were actually fighting troops. These were divided into four combat teams with certain other troops for the defense of beaches and strong points. Eighty per cent of the troops in the Island were native troops, but their equipment, training and morale were of a high standard. It was estimated that 5 or 6 Japanese divisions had been landed.

GENERAL DYXHOORN then said that the Dutch forces were still in a position at least to deal heavy blows to the Japanese forces which were landing. All the Dutch troops were acting offensively in an attempt to drive the Japanese out and only as a last resort would they fall back on the final defensive position around Bandoeng, which town was situated in a plain surrounded by hills some 2,000 feet high.

In reply to a question from General Arnold, GENERAL DYXHOORN said that to the best of his knowledge the Dutch High Command in Java were in touch with General Brett in Australia on the subject of the air reinforcements.

GENERAL ARNOLD pointed out that if the 36 pursuit aircraft landed from the SEAWITCH could be assembled, they should be able to defend at least one aerodrome from which heavy bombers could operate.

2. DEMARKATION OF NEW STRATEGIC AREAS IN THE JAPANESE WAR ZONE.
    (C.C.S. 53)

It was agreed that consideration should be given only to the line dividing the Indian Ocean Area, a British sphere of responsibility, from the Pacific Ocean Area, a U.S. sphere of responsibility.

After a full discussion,

U. S. SECRET
BRITISH MOST SECRET

THE COMMITTEE:-

(a) Agreed that the dividing line between the Indian Ocean and Pacific Ocean Areas should run from Singapore south to the north coast of Sumatra, thence round the east coast of Sumatra (leaving the Sunda Strait to the eastward of the line) to a point on the coast of Sumatra longitude 104° east, thence south to latitude 8° south, thence to Onslow in Australia, thence south along the coast of Australia to longitude 117° east, thence due south.

(b) To defer consideration of the other boundaries of the ABDA Area and of the system of command in the ABDA and adjacent areas.

3. REINFORCEMENT OF AUSTRALIA BY 12 HEAVY BOMBERS.
(C.C.S. 49)

AIR MARSHAL EVILL pointed out that in view of the dependence of this unit on the R.A.A.F. for ground personnel, the question of their command should be settled locally between General Brett, Admiral Leary, and the R.A.A.F.

AIR MARSHAL EVILL reminded the Committee of the serious shortage of aircraft available to Coastal Command and expressed the hope that the replacement of the 12 aircraft diverted from the Coastal Command would be made at the earliest possible date.

GENERAL ARNOLD pointed out that General Brett had authority to arrange for the employment of these aircraft and reassured Air Marshal Evill as to the replacement at an early date of the 12 heavy bombers taken from British allocations.

THE COMMITTEE:-

Accepted the recommendations contained in C.C.S. 49.

U. S. SECRET
BRITISH MOST SECRET

4. AIR TRANSPORTATION FOR MAINTENANCE OF FORCES IN BURMA.
   (C.C.S. 52)

GENERAL ARNOLD explained that at present 38 transport aircraft were operating between Takoradi and Calcutta. It was intended that this number should shortly be increased to 104 and these aircraft would be used mainly for building up the U.S. forces operating in India and Burma. The cutting of the Burma Road had, however, necessitated planning for the employment of an additional 100 transport planes which could be used for taking vital supplies to China. He had already taken 25 transport aircraft from commercial air lines in the U.S. and an officer was now in China studying the facilities available for the operation of aircraft between India and Chungking. Rather than divert transport aircraft to the British, he would prefer that the British should use the existing U.S. facilities thus avoiding duplication of services where possible.

AIR MARSHAL EVILL mentioned the purely British problem of the maintenance of British forces operating in Burma.

GENERAL ARNOLD said that he would welcome the appointment of a British officer to the Air Transport Staff in Washington.

AIR MARSHAL EVILL explained that he was already making arrangements to obtain the services of an officer from the Middle East well versed in local air transport problems. The Air Officer Commanding in Cairo had also asked for a United States officer to be appointed to his staff to deal with coordination of air transport services through the Middle East.

GENERAL ARNOLD said that he had already appointed such an officer.

THE COMMITTEE:-

Took note of the measures being taken by the U.S. to increase air transport facilities in India and Burma which would be available both for British and U.S. use.

U. S. SECRET
BRITISH MOST SECRET

5. ASSIGNMENT OF MUNITIONS, GROUND FORCES.
    (C.C.S. 50)

ADMIRAL KING said that he felt that the ideas expressed in the paper under consideration would be of great use to the Combined Munitions Assignments Board in assisting them to apply the basic strategic guidance which should be given them. This guidance, however, had not yet been produced.

GENERAL MARSHALL outlined the serious situation with regard to equipment of U.S. troops which had been disclosed by a study which the Staff had recently made. The requirements of defense aid, more particularly that necessitated by the Russian Protocol, had caused a very serious situation. There were in existence 30 U.S. divisions which had been formed for over a year. The majority of these had only 50 per cent equipment, and the study he referred to had disclosed the fact that there would be no chance of equipping these 30 divisions fully by March, which was the tentative date originally proposed. He had then ordered a calculation to be made as to the number of divisions which available tonnage would enable to operate overseas in 1942. Fourteen divisions, it was found, could be maintained overseas, but even if only these divisions were equipped and the date of equipment delayed from March until June, there would still be many critical items which could not be made available for them.

GENERAL MARSHALL then presented a memorandum* which General Aurand had prepared as a guide showing the strategic background required by the Combined Munitions Assignments Board, from the Combined Chiefs of Staff, to enable them to allocate production on a strategic basis.

A brief study of this document showed that the proposals contained in it closely resembled those in paragraph 5 of C.C.S. 50.

*Subsequently circulated as M.B.W. 3.

U. S. SECRET
BRITISH MOST SECRET

GENERAL WEMYSS pointed out that the necessary strategic policy had not been provided for the Combined Munitions Assignments Board. The two papers concerned were designed to provide an adequate mechanism to enable the Combined Munitions Assignments Board to implement strategic policy and to suggest in what form strategic guidance could most usefully be given.

THE COMMITTEE:-

Agreed to refer both memoranda to the Munitions Assignments Board for consideration, and to instruct the Board to report to the Combined Chiefs of Staff the precise nature and form of the strategic guidance required by them from the Combined Staff Planners.

6. DEFENSE OF THE CAUCASUS.
(C.C.S. 51 and C.C.S. 54)

SIR JOHN DILL outlined the British forces available in the Middle East area prior to the entry of Japan into the war, the present forces available, and the proposed reinforcements.

THE COMMITTEE:-

(a) Agreed that a German attempt to gain the Caucasus this year was probable.

(b) Instructed the Secretaries to prepare, in consultation with the British Joint Planning Staff, a memorandum for the President stating the above information and giving a broad outline of what may happen and the measures now in prospect to meet this threat.

7. SUPER GYMNAST
(C.C.S. 5/2)

U. S. SECRET
BRITISH MOST SECRET

    THE COMMITTEE:-

    Agreed in principle with the recommendations contained in this paper, but decided to defer its presentation to the President and Prime Minister for one week, pending further consideration of the best method of so doing.

U. S. SECRET
BRITISH MOST SECRET

C.C.S. 10th Meeting.

COMBINED CHIEFS OF STAFF

MINUTES of Meeting held in Room 240,
Public Health Building, on Saturday, March
7, 1942, at 3:30 p.m.

PRESENT

Admiral H. R. Stark, USN
General G. C. Marshall, USA
Admiral E. J. King, USN
Lt. General H. H. Arnold, USA

Field Marshal Sir John Dill
Admiral Sir Charles Little
Lt. General Sir Colville Wemyss
Air Marshal D. C. S. Evill

THE FOLLOWING WERE ALSO PRESENT

Rear Admiral J.H. Towers, USN
Rear Admiral R.K. Turner, USN
Captain F. C. Denebrink, USN
Colonel T. T. Handy, USA
Commander R. E. Libby, USN

Lt. Colonel G. K. Bourne

SECRETARIAT

Brig. Gen. W.B. Smith, USA
Commander L.R. McDowell, USN
Commander R.D. Coleridge, RN
Major C. M. Berkeley

U. S. SECRET
BRITISH MOST SECRET

1. MESSAGE FROM THE PRIME MINISTER ON THE CURRENT SITUATION.
(C.C.S. 56 and C.C.S. 56/1)

The Committee had before them a draft reply to the Prime Minister prepared by the Combined Staff Planners for submission from the Combined Chiefs of Staff to the President.

In the course of discussion certain amendments were made to the draft contained in C.C.S.56/1.

THE COMMITTEE:-

Agreed to submit the draft reply as amended in discussion* to the President.

*Annex to these Minutes.

2. BASES IN THE INDIAN OCEAN.

ADMIRAL LITTLE stressed the importance of the bases needed to implement the strategic policy outlined by the Combined Chiefs of Staff in their draft reply to the Prime Minister's telegram to the President. He proposed to produce a short paper for the consideration of the Combined Chiefs of Staff on the present position with regard to bases in the Indian Ocean.

ADMIRAL KING stressed the point that the Combined Chiefs of Staff should not be overburdened with detail but that they should deal only with the broad distribution of forces and priority with regard to the allocation of material.

THE COMMITTEE:-

Took note that the Representatives of the British Chiefs of Staff would prepare a short paper on the subject of bases in the Indian Ocean.

U. S. SECRET
BRITISH MOST SECRET

3.   GOVERNMENTAL AND STRATEGICAL CONTROL AND COMMANDS IN THE ANZAC AREA.
(C.C.S. 57)

GENERAL MARSHALL said that the United States Chiefs of Staff had already given considerable thought to the problem of command in the southwest Pacific. It was fully realized that the Australians were fearful of a quick attack on their territory and that they felt that the present command was unorganized.

SIR JOHN DILL said that the problem was primarily one for the United States to decide on as the areas concerned were all within the United States strategic sphere of responsibility. As, however, the proposals contained in C.C.S. 57 had been put by the Australian and New Zealand Governments to the Prime Minister and these proposals were, he understood, to be discussed at a meeting of the Pacific War Council on Tuesday, March 10, 1942, the British Chiefs of Staff were most anxious to have the views of the United States Chiefs of Staff in order that they could better advise the Prime Minister on the line he should adopt. He personally felt that the whole Pacific Area was one naval command and that it might be unwise to impose a Supreme Commander between the Commander in Chief of the United States Fleet and the naval commands.

ADMIRAL KING said that he was not inclined to favor the proposals which, if put into effect, would cut across the whole system of command and operations of the United States Pacific Fleet.

THE COMMITTEE:-

Took note that if possible the United States Chiefs of Staff would advise the Representatives of the British Chiefs of Staff of their views on these proposals on or before Monday, March 8, 1942.

U. S. SECRET
BRITISH MOST SECRET

ANNEX to Minutes C.C.S. 10th Meeting,
Public Health Building, on
Saturday, March 7, 1942, at 3:30 p.m.

TO FORMER NAVAL PERSON:

1. We have been in constant conference since receipt of your message of March 4, 1942 to insure that nothing is left unexplored which can in any way improve our present prospects. We recognize fully the magnitude of the problems confronting you in the Indian Ocean and are equally concerned over those which confront us in the Pacific, particularly since the United States assumes a heavy responsibility regarding measures for the defense of Australia, New Zealand, and the guarding of their sea approaches. You, on the other hand, will recognize the difficulties under which we labor in deploying and maintaining, in unprepared and distant positions, the considerable forces which will be required to meet this critical situation. I know that you will also appreciate that success in holding this region depends largely upon the adequacy of shipping, and the availability of munitions and aircraft for arming Dominion forces. The magnitude of the effort which may be put forth by the United States in the southwest Pacific has a direct relation to the magnitude of the air offensive which the United States will be able to undertake from United Kingdom bases.

2. The United States is now operating a large part of the Pacific Fleet in the ANZAC region, for the defense of Australia and New Zealand, for preserving a base area for a future decisive offensive against Japan, and for containing Japanese naval and air forces in the Pacific. Provided their bases in the west of Australia can be kept secure, U.S. submarines will continue to operate in the ABDA Area against Japanese supply lines and against naval forces that exit to the Indian Ocean.

3. While Japan is indeed extending herself over a large area, it must be admitted that the deployment has been skilfully executed and continues to be effective. The energy of the Japanese attack is still very powerful. It is only through a greater energy, skill, and deter-

U. S. SECRET
BRITISH MOST SECRET

mination, that Japan can be halted before she attains a dominating position from which it would prove most difficult to eject her. The United States agrees that the Pacific situation is now very grave, and, if it is to be stabilized, requires an immediate, concerted, and vigorous effort by the United States, Australia, and New Zealand. To establish the many defended bases now planned and to transport to them their garrisons, together with enough amphibious troops for even minor offensives, requires the movement there of some of our amphibious forces, and the use of all our combat loaded transports which are not urgently needed at home for elementary training of additional amphibious formations. The loan to the British of transports for further troop movements to India requires the use of combat transports for carrying U.S. garrisons to positions in the Pacific, and thus seriously reduces present possibilities of offensive action in other regions.

4.   We concur in your estimate of the importance of the Indian and Middle East Areas and agree that reinforcements are required. We also agree that the Australian and New Zealand divisions now in that region should remain. The 41st Division is leaving the United States by the 18th of this month, reaching Australia about April 10, 1942. As a replacement for Australian and New Zealand divisions allotted to the Middle East and India, the United States is prepared to dispatch two additional divisions; one to Australia and one to New Zealand. A convoy of one half a division could leave about April 15, 1942 and the remainder of this division about May 15, 1942. Another U.S. division can also leave for the southwest Pacific about May 15, 1942. It should be understood that our willingness to dispatch these two divisions, over and above the 41st, which is already set up to go, is based on the necessity for economizing in shipping and the continuing security of the Middle East, India and Ceylon. It is, therefore, dependent upon the retention of a similar number of Australian and New Zealand divisions in those theaters. The above movements in the southwest Pacific can be accomplished provided that some twenty-five cargo ships are withdrawn for one voyage from those engaged in transport of Lend-Lease material to the Red Sea and to China, and scheduled to sail in April and May.

U. S. SECRET
BRITISH MOST SECRET

5.   The United States can furnish shipping to move two divisions (40,000 men) with their equipment from the U.K. to the Middle East and India. The first convoy consisting of all the U.S. shipping and the AQUITANIA can depart for U.K. about April 26, 1942 and the remainder about May 6, 1942. The supplying of these ships is contingent upon acceptance of the following during the period they are so used:

(a) GYMNAST cannot be undertaken.

(b) Movements of U.S. troops to the British Isles will be limited to those which these ships can take from the United States.

(c) Direct movements to Iceland (C) cannot be made.

(d) Eleven cargo ships must be withdrawn from sailings for Burma and Red Sea during April and May. These ships are engaged in transportation of Lend-Lease material to China and the Middle East.

(e) American contribution to an air offensive against Germany in 1942 would be somewhat curtailed and any American contribution to land operations on the continent of Europe in 1942 will be materially reduced.

It is considered essential that the U.S. ships used for the movement of the two British divisions be returned to the United States upon completion of the movement.

6.   In addition to considerable U. S. air, antiaircraft and auxiliary troops, there is now in Australia one division, intended for defense of New Caledonia, which contributes directly to Australian security. As stated above, the 41st Division is scheduled to sail to Australia on March 18, 1942. With the arrival of this division, U.S. ground and air forces in Australia and New Caledonia will total some 90,000 men.

Samoa has been garrisoned and a U.S. pursuit squadron has been

U. S. SECRET
BRITISH MOST SECRET

sent to Suva. With the line from Samoa to Australia held, New Zealand in its retired position south thereof, is not thought to be in danger of serious attack.

7. PERSONNEL SHIPPING.

The present shipbuilding program seems to be about the maximum that can be attained, and any increases would not be available until after June, 1944. Included in the program are thirty C-4 ships, each having a lift of 3,675 men, and twenty P-2 ships, each having a lift of 5,750 men. Thus, under construction we now have troopships that will carry 225,250 men. It is understood that the British do not plan to increase their total of troop-carrying ships.

Shipping now available, under the U.S. flag, will lift a total of about 130,000 men. Increases from conversions during 1942 are estimated at at least 35,000 men. By June, 1943, new construction will give an additional 40,000, by December, 1943, an additional 100,000, and by June, 1944, an additional 95,000. Thus, neglecting losses, the total troop carrying capacity of U.S. vessels by June, 1944, will be 400,000 men.

8. AIR.

The deployment of the American air forces, which, at this stage, must be regarded as wholly tentative, including Army and shore based Naval aviation, will be in accordance with the following strategic concept: offense against Germany using maximum forces; defense of the general area, Alaska, Hawaii, Australia, using necessary forces in support of the United States Navy in that area and in maintaining essential sea communications in all U.S. areas; defense of North and South America using essential forces. Tentative distribution by the end of 1942 of first line strength is as follows:

(a) ALASKA, Army one group heavy bombers (35) and one group pursuit (80); Navy 48 VPB

U. S. SECRET
BRITISH MOST SECRET

(b) HAWAII AND NORTH PACIFIC ISLANDS, Army two groups heavy bombers (70), three groups plus two squadrons pursuit (290), one squadron light bombers (13); Navy 126 VPB, 48 VSO, 90 VF, 90 VSB.

(c) SOUTHWEST PACIFIC AND AUSTRALIA, Army two groups heavy bombers (70), two groups medium bombers (114), one group light bombers (57), five groups and one squadron pursuit (425), Navy 90 VPB, 24 VSO, 81 VSB, 81 VF.

(d) CARIBBEAN AREA, Army two groups heavy bombers (70), one group medium bombers (57), one group light bombers (57), four groups pursuit (320); Navy 108 VPB, 60 VSO.

(e) CHINA-INDIA-BURMA AREA, Army one group plus two squadrons heavy bombers (60), one group pursuit (80) exclusive of AVG.

(f) OUTPOSTS ON LINES OF COMMUNICATIONS, Army one squadron of heavy bombers (8), two squadrons medium bombers (26), seven squadrons pursuit (175); Navy 48 VPB, 12 VSO.

(g) ARMY AIR FORCES AVAILABLE FOR OFFENSIVE AGAINST GERMANY:

    (1) JULY 1942, three groups heavy bombers (105), one group medium bombers (57), three groups light bombers (171), five groups pursuit* (400).

    (2) OCTOBER 1942, eleven groups heavy bombers (385), three groups medium bombers (171), five groups light bombers (285), seven groups pursuit* (560).

    (3) JANUARY 1943, fifteen groups heavy bombers (525), seven groups medium bombers (399), seven groups light bombers (399), thirteen groups pursuit* (1040).

* Pursuit to be used as fighter escort for daylight bombing and for offensive sweeps.

U. S. SECRET
BRITISH MOST SECRET

9. This does not include airplanes in depot reserve and those essential for operational training. As much as possible of this force is essential in the United Kingdom if a concerted offensive against German military strength and resources is to be made in 1942. The above dispositions include forces previously set up for GYMNAST and MAGNET.

10. In confiding thus fully and personally to you the details of our military arrangements I do not mean that they should be withheld from your close military advisors. I request, however, that further circulation be drastically reduced.

U. S. SECRET
BRITISH MOST SECRET

C.C.S. 11th Meeting.

COMBINED CHIEFS OF STAFF

MINUTES of Meeting held in Room 240,
Public Health Building, on Tuesday, March
10, 1942, at 2:30 p.m.

PRESENT

Admiral H. R. Stark, USN	Field Marshal Sir John Dill
Admiral E. J. King, USN	Admiral Sir Charles Little
Lt. General H. H. Arnold, USA	Lt. Gen. Sir Colville Wemyss
	Air Marshal D. C. S. Evill

THE FOLLOWING WERE ALSO PRESENT

Rear Admiral R. Willson, USN	Captain J. A. Grindle, RN
Rear Admiral J.H. Towers, USN	For First Part of Meeting:
Rear Admiral R.K. Turner, USN	Maj. Gen. A.Q.H. Dyxhoorn, RNA
Brig. Gen. D. Eisenhower, USA	Representative COSC
Captain Oscar Smith, USN	Admiral J.E.M. Ranneft, RNN
Captain F. C. Denebrink, USN	Dutch Naval Attache
Colonel T. T. Handy, USA	Col. F.G.L. Weijerman, RNIA
Commander R. E. Libby, USN	Dutch Military Attache
Major J. C. Holmes, USA	

ABSENT

General G. C. Marshall, USA

SECRETARIAT

Brigadier V. Dykes
Brig. Gen. W.B. Smith, USA
Commander L.R. McDowell, USN
Commander R.D. Coleridge, RN

U.S. SECRET
BRITISH MOST SECRET

1. SITUATION IN THE N.E.I.

GENERAL DYXHOORN outlined the operations in Java from the 3rd to the 7th of March. Since this latter date no communications had been received from Java. There was no truth in the statement that 98,000 Dutch troops had surrendered. Total forces in Java had only amounted to 60,000 men, including non-combatants, and Dutch forces had dissolved into small guerrilla parties who were continuing to harry the Japanese.

ADMIRAL LITTLE said that it was now presumed that the EXETER, PERTH, ENCOUNTER, STRONGHOLD and two sloops had been lost.

ADMIRAL KING said that no news had been heard of the HOUSTON since the night action in the Sunda Straits.

ADMIRAL RANNEFT then gave details of Dutch naval losses and of the Dutch surface craft and submarines which are at or en route to Colombo.

2. THE SITUATION IN BURMA.

SIR JOHN DILL gave details of the present situation in Burma, including the fact that British forces were withdrawing from Rangoon and demolitions were being carried out in that city. General Alexander had now taken over command of the British forces in Burma.

(At this point, GENERAL DYXHOORN, ADMIRAL RANNEFT and COLONEL WEIJERMAN left the meeting).

3. U.S. AIRCRAFT ALLOCATED TO THE N.E.I.

GENERAL ARNOLD said that some 500 United States aircraft were scheduled for delivery to the N.E.I. This included medium and light bombers, P-40 fighters and transport planes. A few were already en route to the N.E.I.

ADMIRAL KING said that he felt that the movement of these air-

U. S. SECRET
BRITISH MOST SECRET

craft towards Australia should be maintained as they could be used in Australia in lieu of aircraft which the British had undertaken to provide for the Australians.

AIR MARSHAL EVILL agreed with this view and pointed out that the Australians had asked for 250 fighters and that they had many squadrons with good crews but obsolescent aircraft.

THE COMMITTEE:-

Agreed that the United States aircraft scheduled for delivery to the N.E.I. should continue to be moved into Australia and that the manning of these aircraft could be decided on later when it became known what pilots, Australian, Dutch and American, were available to man them.

4. GOVERNMENTAL AND STRATEGICAL CONTROL AND COMMANDS IN THE ANZAC AREA.
(C.C.S. 57) and

DEMARKATION OF NEW STRATEGIC AREAS IN THE JAPANESE WAR ZONE.
(C.C.S. 53)

It was agreed that no further consideration should be given to these two papers pending the answer to the President's telegram of March 9, 1942, to the Prime Minister on the subject of the coordination of the strategic direction of the war by the United Kingdom and the United States.

5. SUPER GYMNAST.
(Previous Reference: C.C.S. 9th Meeting, Minute 7, C.C.S. 5/2)

It was agreed that in view of the Prime Minister's telegram to the President it was unnecessary for the Combined Chiefs of Staff to present any paper to the President or Prime Minister on the subject of Super Gymnast.

U. S. SECRET
BRITISH MOST SECRET

6. BRITISH TROOPS IN JAVA.

ADMIRAL STARK read out a message to the Combined Chiefs of Staff which he had received from General Dyxhoorn stating that the Dutch Commander in Chief of the N.E.I. had informed him that the report stating that British troops had unnecessarily withdrawn from certain positions was entirely unfounded and expressing his deepest apologies for this slight on brave men.

THE COMMITTEE:-

Took note of the above.

7. SITUATION IN NEW GUINEA.

SIR JOHN DILL reminded the Committee of recent reports on Japanese action in New Guinea and New Britain. The Australian Chiefs of Staff felt that an attack on Port Moresby might be expected any time after the middle of March by Japanese aircraft carriers and transports supported by shore based aircraft from New Guinea and New Britain. Such an attack if successful would give them a jumping off ground for a further attack on the east coast of Australia or New Caledonia in April.

ADMIRAL KING then outlined certain operations by United States cruiser carrier groups now taking place in that Area.

8. JAPANESE INTENTIONS.

A discussion took place on the next action likely to be undertaken by the Japanese. It was generally felt that the Japanese would be unable to make major attacks both against India and Australia simultaneously. Both Sir John Dill and Admiral Little stressed the dangers attendant on a Japanese attack on Ceylon which if successful would give them a base from which they could dominate the Indian Ocean.

ADMIRAL TOWERS suggested the possibility of a raid on the fleet base at Colombo similar to that undertaken against Pearl Harbor.

U. S. SECRET
BRITISH MOST SECRET

SIR JOHN DILL then handed to the United States Chiefs of Staff a memorandum which he had prepared on the lines of attack from Burma into India and on the British forces, both land and air, now in India, together with planned reinforcements.

9. SITUATION IN THE MIDDLE EAST.

ADMIRAL STARK initiated a discussion of the importance of the Middle East by asking Sir John Dill what his opinion was as to the relative importance of the Middle East and the Far East.

SIR JOHN DILL reminded the Committee of our present weaknesses in that theater. Forces, both land and air, had been withdrawn for the Far East and India and the British would now be unable to afford Turkey all the support which, in the event of a German drive through Anatolia, we had hoped to be able to provide her. General Rommel's present inactivity in Libya might be due to the fact that he was waiting for reinforcements or he might be waiting to strike as one half of a pincer movement which the Germans might develop on the Canal.

ADMIRAL STARK stated that in his opinion the loss of the Middle East would be much more serious to the United Nations than the loss of the Far East. He said the Middle East was the one place where Germany could be fought. The loss of the Mediterranean and Middle East positions could have tremendous consequences due to its effect on the Moslem world. He had held these views for over two years and had expressed them frequently to the Committee.

ADMIRAL KING also stressed the importance of the Middle East position.

SIR JOHN DILL agreed with these views.

ADMIRAL STARK asked how people in the United Kingdom felt on this subject, as there were people in the United States who held the opinion that the Far East was of greater importance.

U. S. SECRET
BRITISH MOST SECRET

SIR JOHN DILL said that there had been some in the United Kingdom who felt that the Far East was of greater importance. In the earlier part of the war he had himself looked upon the United Kingdom, the Middle East and the Far East as three points upon which British security rested. The loss of the middle point meant that the bridge sagged but the loss of either the United Kingdom or the Far East, more particularly Singapore, meant a much more serious collapse. Now, with Singapore lost, the importance of the Middle East had enormously increased, and he hoped that when Admiral Stark arrived in London, he would not hesitate to express his opinions freely on this matter.

THE COMMITTEE:-

Took note of the above statements.

U. S. SECRET
BRITISH MOST SECRET

C.C.S. 12th Meeting

COMBINED CHIEFS OF STAFF

MINUTES of Meeting held in Room 240, Public Health Building, on Tuesday, March 17, 1942, at 2:30 p.m.

PRESENT

General G.C. Marshall, USA	Field Marshal Sir John Dill
Admiral E.J. King, USN	Admiral Sir Charles Little
Lt. Gen. H. H. Arnold, USA	Lt.Gen. Sir Colville Wemyss
	Air Marshal D.C.S. Evill

THE FOLLOWING WERE ALSO PRESENT

Rear Admiral F. J. Horne, USN	Major Gen. R.H. Dewing
Rear Admiral R. Willson, USN	Lt. Col. G. K. Bourne
Rear Admiral R.K. Turner, USN	
Colonel T. T. Handy, USA	
Captain Oscar Smith, USN	
Captain B. H. Bieri, USN	
Commander R.E. Libby, USN	
Lt. Col. J. C. Holmes, USA	

SECRETARIAT

Brigadier V. Dykes
Brig. Gen. W.B. Smith, USA
Commander L.R. McDowell, USN
Commander R.D. Coleridge, RN

U. S. SECRET
BRITISH MOST SECRET

1. STRATEGIC DIRECTIVE TO GOVERN ASSIGNMENT OF MUNITIONS.
   (C.C.S. 50/1)

GENERAL MARSHALL pointed out that it was suggested that as a first step the Combined Staff Planners should produce an interim report covering Items (a), (b) and (c) of paragraph 2 of the paper.

Both Admiral Turner and Colonel Handy felt that to produce the strategic guidance required by the Munitions Assignments Board in the form in which it had been asked would present a difficult problem which would take too long to accomplish, and suggested that it should be discussed between the Combined Staff Planners and members of the Munitions Assignments Board in order that a simpler and quicker method of producing the strategic guidance might be found.

GENERAL WEMYSS suggested that the problem might be simplified, firstly if the Army, Navy and Air could be considered separately and secondly, if the problem could be considered under two heads:

(a) The normal theaters over which the Combined Chiefs of Staff had direct control, and

(b) Special cases, such as Russia, where diplomatic agreements, or political considerations, were the predominant factor.

THE COMMITTEE:-

Instructed the Combined Staff Planners to discuss with members of the Munitions Assignments Board the problem of providing the necessary strategic guidance in a form which, while satisfactory to the Munitions Assignments Board, could be more easily produced by the Combined Staff Planners.

2. POSSIBLE JAPANESE ACTION AGAINST AUSTRALIA AND NEW ZEALAND.
   (C.C.S. 18/1)

U. S. SECRET
BRITISH MOST SECRET

THE COMMITTEE:-

Took note of this paper.

3. ARRIVAL OF GENERAL MacARTHUR IN AUSTRALIA.

GENERAL MARSHALL gave a brief account of the methods which had been employed in transporting General MacArthur from the Philippines to Australia. The United States Chiefs of Staff had felt great concern as to the adverse effect on the morale of the troops defending the Philippines, and also on possible Axis propaganda based on General MacArthur's move from the Philippines. General Marshall emphasized the difficulties of the task now confronting General Wainwright who had assumed command in the Philippines, particularly in view of the fact that the Japanese were obviously building up strong forces for an offensive.

SIR JOHN DILL, on behalf of the representatives of the British Chiefs of Staff congratulated the United States Chiefs of Staff on the successful evacuation of General MacArthur and his staff and warmly welcomed his appointment as Supreme Commander in Australia.

THE COMMITTEE:-

Took note of the above statements.

4. RELATION OF MERCHANT SHIPPING LOSSES TO THE PROSECUTION OF THE WAR.
(C.C.S. 39/1)

SIR JOHN DILL pointed out that in paragraph 1 (a) (2) and 1 (b) (2) of the above paper, the losses included British, allied, and neutral shipping. He had that morning been informed that the figures of losses for the first ten weeks of the year were now available and that they were at the rate of approximately 7 million gross tons. He felt, however, that this high rate of loss was due in some measure to the marine risks to be expected at this time of the year, and to the losses in the operations around Java.

U. S. SECRET
BRITISH MOST SECRET

ADMIRAL KING agreed that the rate of loss might be expected to decrease, particularly when more resources were available to combat the menace, and the longer hours of daylight in summer would also assist the position.

GENERAL MARSHALL mentioned the use now being made of civilian aircraft for coastal patrols, which it was hoped would be of assistance in reducing shipping losses on the eastern seaboard of America. He suggested that C.C.S. 39/1 should be referred back to the Combined Military Transportation Committee for continuous study with a view to finding, whenever possible, further tonnage for troop movements.

THE COMMITTEE:

Instructed the Combined Military Transportation Committee to keep the shipping position under constant review with the object of finding, whenever possible, additional tonnage for the transportation of troops and combat material.

5. MOVEMENT OF AIRCRAFT AND AIR FORMATIONS.

SIR JOHN DILL said that he had been informed that considerable economy in shipping space would be achieved if, instead of shipping complete air units to an overseas theater, aircraft and spares, together with the necessary pilots, were sent to augment the existing squadrons. The shipping of such aircraft might be achieved at, for instance, the expense of steel required for the U.K. Whereas the steel would not be fabricated into weapons for use before 1943, the shipment of the aircraft in lieu of the steel might assist to hold the position in the difficult days of 1942.

GENERAL MARSHALL felt that there was much to recommend shipping of aircraft to augment existing formations. In Australia, the U.S. were arranging for "overage", both in pilots and aircraft, to keep existing squadrons up to 100 per cent, in spite of heavy wastage. He asked to what extent Australian pilots could be provided to man U.S. aircraft in Australia, and if these pilots were available he felt that they

U. S. SECRET
BRITISH MOST SECRET

should be used both in Australia and New Zealand to man U.S. aircraft already there.

GENERAL ARNOLD said that 50 planes had already been turned over by General Brett to Australian pilots.

AIR MARSHAL EVILL said that his impression was that there was a surplus of pilots in Australia over and above those required to man the modern aircraft available, and therefore considerable local expansion would be possible. He was not very certain to what extent the U.K. were relying on trained pilots from Australia. Two officers were shortly arriving from the U.K. who had full knowledge of this problem, and he would consult further with General Arnold as soon as they had arrived.

Discussion then turned on the importance of reinforcing the air forces in the Middle East. The U.S. Chiefs of Staff presented a memorandum* containing a proposal that U.S. personnel for certain formations should be shipped to the Middle East where they would man certain British aircraft on order in the United States, the necessary war equipment for which should be fitted either before leaving America or on arrival in the Middle East.

AIR MARSHAL EVILL said that it appeared that the limiting factor, both for the U.K. and for the U.S., was shortage of aircraft. The Chief of the Air Staff was most anxious that the first two of the four U.S. pursuit groups scheduled to go to the U.K. should be diverted to the Middle East.

GENERAL ARNOLD pointed out that acceptance of this proposal was dependent on a decision on major strategy as to where our main offensive was to take place. Air Marshal Portal had also asked for three light or medium bombardment groups for the Middle East.

AIR MARSHAL EVILL explained that a strong offensive in the Middle East was feared within a month or so, and that, while nothing which was sent now could arrive in time to deal with the initial attack, it would help as a reinforcement to hold the offensive and make good the

*Annex to these minutes.

U. S. SECRET
BRITISH MOST SECRET

heavy wastage which must be expected.

    THE COMMITTEE:-

        (a)   Took note that General Arnold and Air Marshal Evill would consider, in the light of discussion, the question of how best air assistance might be rendered to the Middle East.

        (b)   Took note that the Representatives of the British Chiefs of Staff would refer the proposals contained in the U.S. Chiefs of Staff memorandum to London.

6.   COMMAND IN ICELAND.
    (C.C.S. 58)

SIR JOHN DILL said that the War Office was most anxious that the remaining 9,000 men of the 49th Division should, if possible, be taken out of Iceland. They had gone there from Norway and had already spent two winters in the Island. Would it not be possible for them to be relieved by U.S. troops carried there in the shipping which had been offered to convey the 40,000 British troops to the Middle East?

COLONEL HANDY explained that General Chaney was particularly anxious to get the U.S. armored division into Northern Ireland, and that the possibility of relieving the 9,000 British troops in Iceland was dependent on the type of formations to be taken to Northern Ireland, as well as on the port facilities available in Iceland.

GENERAL MARSHALL said that if it were found to be possible he was in favor of the British troops in Iceland being relieved.

ADMIRAL KING reminded the Committee of the acute shortage of U.S. escort vessels in the Atlantic.

ADMIRAL LITTLE offered to communicate with the Admiralty with a view to British vessels providing some relief.

U. S. SECRET
BRITISH MOST SECRET

With regard to the naval position in Iceland, he was endeavoring to expedite a reply from the Admiralty on the points which he had previously discussed with Admiral King.

GENERAL MARSHALL asked that the question of command in Iceland could be deferred until the U.S. Chiefs of Staff had had time to consider it.

THE COMMITTEE:-

(a) Instructed the Combined Military Transportation Committee to examine the possibility of arranging for the relief of the British troops in Iceland and for their transportation to the U.K.

(b) Took note that the U.S. Chiefs of Staff would inform the representatives of the British Chiefs of Staff on the question of command in Iceland.

7. PRESIDENT'S PROPOSALS ON THE DIVISION OF STRATEGIC RESPONSIBILITY.

It was explained that in general the proposals which the President had transmitted to the Prime Minister, and to which a reply was expected in the next 24 hours, were that there should be three main theaters of operations: The Pacific as far west as Singapore, a U.S. responsibility; the Indian Ocean and Middle East, a British responsibility; and the Atlantic, including Europe, which would be a joint responsibility. Within the Pacific Ocean the U.S. Chiefs of Staff proposed that there should be a Southwest Pacific Area to include the old ABDA Area east of Sumatra and Singapore, the Philippines, the Commonwealth of Australia, New Guinea and the Solomons and a strip of ocean to the eastward of Australia. In addition, there would be a South Pacific Area which would include New Caledonia, New Zealand, Fiji and Samoa, and would be an area covering the strategic line of communications to Australia. The Southwest Pacific Area would be under the supreme command of General MacArthur and the naval forces would probably be under Admiral

U. S. SECRET
BRITISH MOST SECRET

Leary, and would include the Australian Squadron and what was left of the U.S. Asiatic Fleet. The South Pacific Area would be a naval command and would include the New Zealand Squadron.

ADMIRAL KING stressed the difficulties and delays which would undoubtedly arise if the Pacific War Council remained in London rather than in Washington. The area for which they were responsible would be a U.S. area and the Military decisions could be taken only in Washington. With regard to the formalization of General MacArthur's position, it was generally agreed that this must await the receipt of the Prime Minister's reply to the President's proposals. In the meantime, General Marshall and Admiral King had jointly informed General Brett, Admiral Leary, and Admiral Glassford of the tentative arrangements which the U.S. Chiefs of Staff proposed for the Southwest Pacific Area.

THE COMMITTEE:-

Took note of the above statements.

8.   NAVAL BASES IN THE INDIAN OCEAN.

ADMIRAL LITTLE said that he had prepared a paper on the subject of the naval bases in the Indian Ocean, which, in view of the fact that it contained a certain amount of detail, he did not propose to lay before the Combined Chiefs of Staff, but would arrange for it to be given to the Combined Staff Planners for their information.

THE COMMITTEE -

Took note of the above statement.

- 98 -

U. S. SECRET
BRITISH MOST SECRET

ANNEX 1

PROPOSAL FOR ESTABLISHMENT OF U.S. AIR UNITS IN CAIRO

1.   The Joint U.S. Chiefs of Staff, appreciating the urgency of the British request for air reinforcements to the Cairo area, have explored every means of complying with that request. Our analysis indicates that there is insufficient U.S. aircraft available to meet these requirements, although personnel for the units can be made available. It is proposed that the U.S. undertake to provide the air units, and that the British make available the necessary aircraft from their production in the United States, provide the equipment necessary to make those aircraft operational, and undertake to move the units.

2.   The plan proposed is as follows:

    (a)   The force will consist of:

        (1)   An Air Force Headquarters

        (2)   1 Medium Bombardment Group

        (3)   2 Light Bombardment Groups

        (4)   2 Pursuit Groups

        (5)   Essential Services

    (b)   The United States will furnish all personnel and all equipment except aircraft and aircraft accessories.

    (c)   The British to furnish:

        (1)   60 B-34 (Ventura)(medium bombers) at the earliest possible date, in the United States.

U. S. SECRET
BRITISH MOST SECRET

        These aircraft to be operationally equipped, either here on in Cairo.

    (2) 160 P-40 airplanes (pursuit) to be delivered from stocks in Cairo, set up, and operationally equipped.

    (3) 60 DB-7 airplanes (light bombers) delivered in the United States as soon as possible and operationally equipped, either in the United States or in Cairo.

    (4) 60 Martin 187 airplanes (light bombers) delivered in the United States as soon as possible, and operationally equipped either in the United States or in Cairo

(d) The United States will have units ready for overseas movement as follows:

    (1) Personnel for 2 pursuit groups--April 20, 1942

    (2) Personnel for 2 light bomb groups--six weeks after receipt of total complement of aircraft.

    (3) Personnel for 1 medium bomb group--six weeks after receipt of total complement of aircraft.

(e) Aircraft of the medium bomb group will be flown to Egypt. Other aircraft will be shipped.

(f) Maintenance, supplies, and attrition replacements to be provided from British production.

U. S. SECRET
BRITISH MOST SECRET

C.C.S. 13th Meeting.

COMBINED CHIEFS OF STAFF

MINUTES of meeting held in Room 240,
Combined Chiefs of Staff Building, on Tuesday, March
24, 1942, at 2:30 p.m.

PRESENT

General G. C. Marshall, USA	Field Marshal Sir John Dill
Admiral E. J. King, USN	Admiral Sir Charles Little
Lt. Gen. H. H. Arnold, USA	Air Marshal D.C.S. Evill
	Major General R.H. Dewing

THE FOLLOWING WERE ALSO PRESENT

Vice Admiral F. J. Horne, USN	Air Commodore S.C. Strafford
Vice Admiral R. Willson, USN	
Rear Admiral R.K. Turner, USN	
Colonel T. T. Handy, USA	
Captain Oscar Smith, USN	
Captain B. H. Bieri, USN	
Commander R. E. Libby, USN	
Lt. Col. J. C. Holmes, USA	

SECRETARIAT

Brigadier V. Dykes
Brig. Gen. W.B. Smith, USA
Commander L.R. McDowell, USN
Commander R.D. Coleridge, RN

U. S. SECRET
BRITISH MOST SECRET

1. DEMARKATION OF NEW STRATEGIC AREAS IN THE JAPANESE WAR.
   (C.C.S. 53)

   THE COMMITTEE:-

   Took note that this paper had been superseded.

2. GOVERNMENTAL AND STRATEGICAL CONTROL AND COMMANDS IN THE ANZAC AREA.
   (C.C.S. 57)

   THE COMMITTEE-

   Took note that this paper had been superseded.

3. AUSTRALIAN VIEWS ON STRATEGIC CONTROL IN THE PACIFIC AREA.
   (C.C.S. 57/1)

   ADMIRAL LITTLE explained that he had discussed paragraph (i) of the above paper with Admiral King. The First Sea Lord's proposal for the line of demarkation between the Pacific and Indian Ocean Areas, which was in contradiction to the Australian views, was due to a misunderstanding which he had now cleared up by signal with the First Sea Lord. The First Sea Lord had thought that the naval responsibility for repelling invasion on the northwesterly coast of Australia lay with the British Far Eastern Fleet, but Admiral King had agreed to accept this responsibility and on that understanding Admiral Little felt sure that the British Chiefs of Staff would be prepared to accept the Australian proposal as outlined in paragraph (i) of C.C.S. 57/1, which proposal was also acceptable to Admiral King. The Supreme Commander of the Southwest Pacific Area would therefore cooperate with the British and United States naval forces in the two adjoining areas.

   With regard to the directive to the Supreme Commander in the Southwest Pacific Area it was agreed that this would be issued to General MacArthur by the United States Government in direct consultation as necessary with the Australian Government

U. S. SECRET
BRITISH MOST SECRET

With regard to paragraph (ii) of C.C.S. 57/1, SIR JOHN DILL said that while the Australian arguments in favor of including China in the Indian Ocean Theater rather than the Pacific Theater were logical, it was obvious that for political reasons China must fall within the United States sphere of strategical control. In this connection it was generally agreed that General Stilwell was competing most successfully with his very difficult task.

SIR JOHN DILL mentioned a telegram from General Wavell asking for information on the functions of the Council in Chungking.

GENERAL MARSHALL undertook to ask the President to give his views on the way in which this body would work.

ADMIRAL KING expressed grave concern at the suggestion that there should be two Pacific War Councils, one in London and one in Washington.

SIR JOHN DILL agreed that obvious difficulties would arise and said he realized, as did the British Chiefs of Staff in London, that the control of military operations in the Pacific Area was the responsibility of the United States Chiefs of Staff.

GENERAL MARSHALL said he appreciated that the present difficulties with regard to the proposal that there should be two Pacific War Councils arose largely from the constitutional differences between the British system, whereby the Chiefs of Staff were the military advisers to a small Ministerial body, whereas in the United States the Chiefs of Staff dealt directly with the President as Commander in Chief of the United States Army and Navy.

GENERAL MARSHALL then read out the text of a draft message on the subject of strategic control in the Pacific theater prepared by the United States Chiefs of Staff for the President to send to the Prime Minister. The representatives of the British Chiefs of Staff expressed general agreement with the terms of this draft.

U. S. SECRET
BRITISH MOST SECRET

THE COMMITTEE:—

    (a) Agreed that since naval responsibility for dealing with sea-borne raids on the northwest coast of Australia would lie with the United States, the western boundary of the Southwest Pacific Area should be as follows: from Singapore south to the north coast of Sumatra, thence round the east coast of Sumatra (leaving the Sunda Strait to the eastward of the line) to a point on the coast of Sumatra at longitude 104° east, thence south to latitude 08° south, thence easterly towards Onslow, and on reaching longitude 110° east, due south along that meridian.

    (b) Invited the U.S. Chiefs of Staff to consider the question of the relations between the Chungking Joint Military Council and the Combined Chiefs of Staff, and to inform the representatives of the British Chiefs of Staff of their proposals.

    (c) Took note of the concurrence of the representatives of the British Chiefs of Staff to the terms of the U.S. Chiefs of Staff memorandum to the President on the subject of strategic control in the Pacific theater.

4.   STRATEGIC RESPONSIBILITY OF THE UNITED KINGDOM AND THE UNITED STATES.

    The Committee was informed that it was understood that the proposals contained in the enclosure to C.C.S. 57/2 had been communicated by the President to the Prime Minister, though the exact terms in which this telegram had been couched were not known. The United States Chiefs of Staff desired to have the comments of the British Chiefs of Staff on these proposals.

U. S. SECRET
BRITISH MOST SECRET

THE COMMITTEE:-

Took note that the proposals of the United States Chiefs of Staff for defining the strategic responsibility of the United Kingdom and the United States for the prosecution of the war as a whole, as contained in C.C.S. 57/2, would be referred to London by the representatives of the British Chiefs of Staff.

5. COMMAND IN ICELAND.
    (C.C.S. 58)

GENERAL MARSHALL stated that the United States Chiefs of Staff agreed that command of the island base should pass to the command of the United States Commander when two thirds of the forces in Iceland were American, the actual date of the passing of command to be determined by Generals Bonesteel and Curtis.

GENERAL MARSHALL added that the United States Chiefs of Staff hoped that the British air units now stationed in Iceland would not be withdrawn as there were no United States air units available to relieve them.

AIR MARSHAL EVILL said that there was no intention to withdraw the $2\frac{1}{2}$ British squadrons now operating in Iceland but that he thought that no further air reinforcements would be available from British sources.

THE COMMITTEE:-

(a) Agreed that the command in Iceland would pass to General Bonesteel when two thirds of the forces in the island were American, the actual date to be decided between Generals Bonesteel and Curtis.

(b) Agreed that the British air units now operating in Iceland would not be withdrawn.

U. S. SECRET
BRITISH MOST SECRET

6.   RELIEF OF BRITISH TROOPS IN ICELAND.

GENERAL MARSHALL said that the report contained in C.C.S. 58/1 had now been revised by the Combined Military Transportation Committee and that the new proposal would necessitate approximately 5,000 of the British troops in Iceland leaving their equipment behind for the use of the United States forces until replaced from the United States.

GENERAL MARSHALL then read out an extract from a telegram from the Prime Minister to the President asking that 9,000 British troops in Iceland should be relieved by United States forces. He was in some doubt as to whether this referred to the 9,000 combat troops for which arrangements were being made, or for the relief of a further 9,000 who would consist of coast defense and service troops. It was generally felt that the Prime Minister was probably referring only to the 9,000 combat troops.

ADMIRAL KING said that he hoped that the necessary escorts would be forthcoming but that it would be necessary for him to study the new plan before giving a final answer.

THE COMMITTEE:

(a)   Agreed to consider, and if possible, approve prior to the next meeting, the new plan being forwarded by the Combined Military Transportation Committee*.

(b)   Took note that the representatives of the British Chiefs of Staff would clear up with London the question of whether the Prime Minister was referring to the 9,000 British combat troops in Iceland or to an additional 9,000 troops.

*Subsequently circulated as C.C.S. 58/2.

U. S. SECRET
BRITISH MOST SECRET

7. ASSIGNMENT OF MUNITIONS, APRIL, 1942
(C.C.S. 55)   and

DIRECTIVE FOR ASSIGNMENT OF MUNITIONS.
(C.C.S. 50/2)

GENERAL MARSHALL explained that of the 16 divisions mentioned in paragraph 3 (a) of C.C.S. 55, 12 of these would be equipped up to 100 per cent by March 31, 1942, leaving only 4 divisions to be so equipped by June 30, 1942. At present the United States had 5 divisions overseas and one additional division due to sail in April. Three divisions were earmarked for overseas service and were awaiting shipment. A further 2 divisions were training in amphibious operations.

With regard to the necessity for providing weapons for training, GENERAL MARSHALL stressed the bad effect on morale of the removal of weapons from semi-trained units which had been necessary in order to equip other units for overseas service. This policy, which had proved to be the only practical one, had caused considerable adverse comment both in Congress and the Press.

SIR JOHN DILL said that he felt that the strategic directive (C.C.S. 50/2) produced by the Combined Staff Planners was a very real step forward in relating the assignment of munitions to the strategic concept. He suggested that this report should be used for April allocations and that the Munitions Assignments Board should be asked, in the light of the experience gained in April allocations, to report on any points on which they considered a more detailed direction was necessary. As the views of the Combined Chiefs of Staff on future strategy developed it would be possible to redraft the directive so that it should be more closely related to an agreed strategy.

ADMIRAL KING agreed that the directive constituted an excellent basis for allocations and would serve as a modus vivendi pending future possible revision.

ADMIRAL TURNER pointed out that the United States Planners did

U. S. SECRET
BRITISH MOST SECRET

not feel that the Munitions Assignments Board was a body to whom all our future plans should be revealed. The directive issued to the Board would of course be based on the plans but the plans themselves would not be handed over.

ADMIRAL TURNER added that the appendices which would shortly be added to C.C.S. 50/2 ought, he felt, to be referred to the Combined Chiefs of Staff for their approval as they indicated the scale of effort which it was proposed to devote to each theater.

THE COMMITTEE:-

(a) Agreed to accept C.C.S. 50/2 as a guide directive for the assignment of munitions, to include April assignments, subject to study and revision as the strategic situation changes and policy is developed.

(b) Took note that the directive would be referred to London and that any modifications proposed by the British Chiefs of Staff would be submitted later for consideration.

(c) Agreed to withdraw C.C.S. 55 in consideration of the above.

(d) Instructed the Combined Staff Planners to submit the appendices to C.C.S. 50/2 to the Combined Chiefs of Staff as soon as they were completed.

8. ASCENSION ISLAND.
(C.C.S. 28/1)

THE COMMITTEE:-

Accepted the proposals contained in the Annex to C.C.S. 28/1 as a working agreement to be used pending formal agreement between the Governments of the United Kingdom and the United

U. S. SECRET
BRITISH MOST SECRET

States as to the terms and conditions under which the United States will become responsible for the military defense of Ascension Island.

9. OFFENSIVE OPERATIONS IN EUROPE.

After a brief discussion,

THE COMMITTEE:-

Instructed the Combined Staff Planners to consider the British and United States studies for an offensive in Europe and to report to the Combined Chiefs of Staff on the following lines:

(a) Is it possible to put the ground forces on the Continent during 1942 with sufficient support to give reasonable assurance that they can be maintained there?

(b) Is an invasion of the Continent early in 1943 a possibility? If so, the estimates of the British and American Planning Staffs as to material required should be reconciled.

(c) If the answer to (a) above is in the negative, how does this affect United States participation in or assistance to the British defense of the Middle East in 1942?

10. BRITISH COMBINED OPERATIONS STAFF.

SIR JOHN DILL informed the Committee that certain British officers of the three services were shortly arriving in the United States with the object of studying U.S. practice with regard to combined operations and to pass on all the information they had with regard to British experiences in combined operations. These officers would deal mainly with the tactical and technical problems of combined operations rather than with planning.

U. S. SECRET
BRITISH MOST SECRET

    ADMIRAL KING undertook to arrange, through Admiral Willson, that the British officers should be put in touch with the United States naval and marine officers dealing with this problem, and General Marshall said that arrangements could be made for them to visit the new amphibious training center through which army divisions were being passed.

    THE COMMITTEE:-

Took note of the above statements.

U. S. SECRET
BRITISH MOST SECRET

C.C.S. 14th Meeting.

COMBINED CHIEFS OF STAFF

MINUTES of meeting held in Room 240, Combined Chiefs of Staff Building, on Tuesday, March 31, 1942, at 2:30 p.m.

PRESENT

General G. C. Marshall, USA	Field Marshal Sir John Dill
Admiral E. J. King, USN	Admiral Sir Charles Little
Lt. Gen. H. H. Arnold, USA	Air Marshal D.C.S. Evill
	Major General R.H. Dewing

THE FOLLOWING WERE ALSO PRESENT

Vice Admiral F. J. Horne, USN	For Item 3:
Vice Admiral R. Willson, USN	Wing Comdr. C.McK. Henry, RAAF
Rear Admiral J.H. Towers, USN	
Rear Admiral R.K. Turner, USN	
Brig. Gen. T. T. Handy, USA	
Captain Oscar Smith, USN	
Captain B. H. Bieri, USN	
Commander R. E. Libby, USN	
Lt. Col. J. C. Holmes, USA	

SECRETARIAT

Brigadier V. Dykes
Brig. Gen. W.B. Smith, USA
Commander L.R. McDowell, USN
Commander R.D. Coleridge, RN

U. S. SECRET
BRITISH MOST SECRET

1. STRATEGIC RESPONSIBILITY OF THE UNITED KINGDOM AND THE UNITED STATES.
   (C.C.S. 57/2)

GENERAL MARSHALL explained that some confusion had been caused by the fact that the President had not telegraphed the contents of this paper to the Prime Minister and in the telegram which had been sent had referred to a Supreme Commander in the whole Pacific Area which had not been visualized by the U.S. Chiefs of Staff. In order to clarify the position, the U.S. Chiefs of Staff had, however, drafted proposed directives for the two Supreme Commanders in the Pacific Theater (General MacArthur for the Southwest Pacific Area and Admiral Nimitz for the remainder of the Pacific). If the President approved of these directives then the position would become clearer.

With regard to the political machinery for the higher control of the Pacific Area, GENERAL MARSHALL reminded the Committee that the Pacific War Council in Washington was meeting on the following day but he did not know what subjects would be discussed.

In the course of a discussion on the views of the Australian and New Zealand Governments with regard to the incorporation of both Dominions within the same area, ADMIRAL KING said that he had discussed the question with Dr. Evatt and Mr. Nash, and both appeared to agree with the U.S. proposals whereby they would be in different areas. The views of the Australian and New Zealand Governments appeared to be influenced by an agreement which they had reached whereby each had undertaken to cooperate with the other in the defense of the two Dominions.

SIR JOHN DILL said that the defense of New Zealand rested primarily on sea and air power and that it would in his opinion be an unwise diversion of force to build up strong land forces in New Zealand. He personally felt that New Zealand would be in a stronger position if under the direct command of the Naval Supreme Commander of the Pacific Area.

ADMIRAL KING said that he had pointed out to Mr. Nash the

U. S. SECRET
BRITISH MOST SECRET

relative security enjoyed by New Zealand as long as the fortified line of communication from Hawaii to Australia remained intact.

ADMIRAL KING added that a despatch had been sent to Admiral Leary instructing him to assume command of the U.S. Asiatic Fleet previously under Admiral Glassford in addition to retaining his present command, and place himself at the disposal of General MacArthur to co-operate with him pending formal establishment of unity of command in the area.

THE COMMITTEE:-

Agreed that no further action could be taken on C.C.S. 57/2 until a final decision had been reached on a political level.

2. RELIEF OF BRITISH TROOPS IN ICELAND.
(C.C.S. 58/2)

THE COMMITTEE were informed that agreement had been received from London that the British troops should leave their equipment to be taken over by certain of the U.S. forces going to Iceland.

ADMIRAL KING outlined the escort position whereby the British had agreed to furnish the necessary escort for the second convoy from Iceland to the United Kingdom and the Commander in Chief of the U.S. Atlantic Fleet had been asked to arrange to escort the second convoy as far as Iceland. Though Admiral King had not received specific information of his ability to undertake this, he felt no doubt that it could be accomplished.

ADMIRAL LITTLE said that he had that morning learned that the QUEEN MARY had been ordered back to New York and would be available for this movement.

SIR JOHN DILL said that he presumed this move meant that the 9th Australian Division would remain in the Middle East. He considered this particularly important in view of the difficulties which would

U. S. SECRET
BRITISH MOST SECRET

arise if all Australian troops in the Middle East were withdrawn while New Zealand forces remained.

GENERAL MARSHALL said that in this connection he had suggested to the President that the condition whereby a second United States division was provided for Australia only if the 9th Australian Division remained in the Middle East, should be withdrawn. However, the importance of the 9th Australian Division remaining in the Middle East should be emphasized to the Australian authorities since the removal of these troops would entail a diminution of British strength to the extent of 60,000 men because of the transport involved.

THE COMMITTEE:-

Agreed to accept C.C.S. 58/2.

3. U.S. AIRCRAFT ALLOCATED TO THE N.E.I.
(Previous Reference: C.C.S. 11th Meeting, Item 3)

GENERAL ARNOLD raised the question of the allocation to the Australian area of 611 aircraft previously scheduled for delivery to the Netherlands East Indies. He had discussed this matter with Dr. Evatt and Mr. Casey. The Netherlands authorities had informed him that they required only 18 of these aircraft (for which they had paid cash) in Australia for the present. They wished that the remaining planes should be turned over to the U.S. authorities on the condition that they should be used in the United States for a Dutch training scheme and that the combat types would be replaced late in 1942 or early in 1943 when Dutch pilots would be available to man them. The present position was that only 54 of these aircraft were completed: 18 were already in Australia, 24 were en route, 5 were on their way via India (and as they would be unable to proceed from there to Australia they were being diverted to General Brereton's command), 3 had crashed, and 4 were not yet ready.

SIR JOHN DILL reminded the Committee of the reasons which had led the Combined Chiefs of Staff to decide that the flow of these aircraft to Australia must continue. The defense of Australia was an urgent

U. S. SECRET
BRITISH MOST SECRET

need and crews were available to use them operationally at once.

AIR MARSHAL EVILL said that the Australian authorities were anxious that the flow should continue as trained crews were available in Australia and 8 fully trained operational squadrons were at present equipped with obsolete Wirraways. The value of getting these aircraft into Australia where they could at once be absorbed into formed units was obvious in view of the importance of the time factor. No shipping would be required as the aircraft could be flown out.

ADMIRAL TOWERS suggested that the Dutch contracts for any but completed aircraft should be cancelled and that the U.S. Army and Navy should then take over the contracts and that the Combined Chiefs of Staff should decide in the light of the strategic situation at the time to what theater the remaining planes were to be allocated.

With regard to the training of Australian or Dutch pilots and crews in Australia, GENERAL MARSHALL said that General Brett had informed him that training in Australia could not be increased in view of limited maintenance facilities which were now being largely employed for operational squadrons.

ADMIRAL KING said that he knew of no change of view on the part of the Combined Chiefs of Staff with regard to the necessity for the continued flow of these aircraft to the Australian area.

(At this point, WING COMMANDER HENRY entered the meeting.)

WING COMMANDER HENRY explained that the Dutch had offered these aircraft to the Australians with the proviso that immediate financial arrangements must be made or the contract would be cancelled. He understood that the day after this offer was made a somewhat similar offer was made to the U.S. air forces.

With regard to the availability of Australian pilots, WING COMMANDER HENRY confirmed that 8 complete operational trained squadrons were ready with only obsolete aircraft.

U. S. SECRET
BRITISH MOST SECRET

With regard to arrangements for ferrying the aircraft to Australia he explained that Australian crews trained in England or North America were available to undertake this task though in certain cases the captains of the aircraft would have to be provided from other sources.

In reply to a question as to training facilities in Australia, **WING COMMANDER HENRY** said that though considerable training facilities existed, having been built up in connection with the Empire air scheme, he felt that the largely increased size of the operational air force in Australia would be placing a heavy load on the maintenance facilities.

(At this point WING COMMANDER HENRY left the meeting)

THE COMMITTEE:-

    (a) Took note that the U.S. Chiefs of Staff would reconsider the question of the flow of Dutch aircraft to the Australian Theater and would submit their proposals to the Combined Chiefs of Staff.

    (b) Agreed that pending consideration of the proposals referred to in (a) above, the movement of completed aircraft to Australia should continue.

4.   CONSIDERATION OF U.S.—BRITISH REQUIREMENTS FOR ESCORT VESSELS.

ADMIRAL LITTLE referred to the suggestion that the U.S. Navy might wish to take over certain of the corvettes now building in Canada. He had ascertained that none of these corvettes would be completed until the end of 1942 and that most of them would not be finished until 1943 or even 1944. In this connection he suggested that it might be wise if the Combined U.S.—British Naval Staffs in Washington reviewed the whole problem of the future requirements of the two Navies for corvettes and perhaps destroyers. Such aspects as strategic responsibilities and the manning problem could be reviewed.

ADMIRAL KING welcomed the proposal that the Combined Naval

U. S. SECRET
BRITISH MOST SECRET

Staffs should review the position with regard to corvettes but felt that consideration of the destroyer position should for the present be deferred.

SIR JOHN DILL suggested that the question of both the United States and British building programs for landing craft should also be examined as it appeared that they might prove the limiting factor for any offensive operations.

THE COMMITTEE:-

Agreed that the U.S.--British Naval Staffs in Washington should review and report on the adequacy, in the light of strategic requirements, of the combined building program for corvettes and landing craft.

5. ALLOCATION OF AIR FORCES.

ADMIRAL KING read to the Committee a telegram* from the Prime Minister to the President containing a request for the earliest possible employment from Great Britain of a U.S. bomber force of at least 100 aircraft. The Prime Minister had pointed out the diversion of bombers to anti-submarine work in the Bay of Biscay aimed at lessening the scale of attack on shipping off the east coast of America, and had also informed the President of the unserviceability of certain British heavy bombers. The Prime Minister had stressed the success of recent bomber attacks on Germany but feared that the weight of attack throughout the summer months would fall off instead of increasing.

GENERAL MARSHALL said that he was encouraged by the Prime Minister's telegram in that it reinforced his own views of the importance of a heavy bomber offensive from the United Kingdom. General Marshall reviewed the many demands made for U.S. aircraft which though important in themselves tended to cause a dispersion of effort which he was sure ought to be avoided. In order that the very important decisions as to the allocation of aircraft could be taken in the light of the fullest possible knowledge, he hoped that the Representatives of the British Chiefs of

*No. 60.

U. S. SECRET
BRITISH MOST SECRET

Staff would provide the U.S. Chiefs of Staff with the fullest information as to British aircraft material resources in each theater of war.

GENERAL ARNOLD also stressed the importance of operating U.S. heavy bombers from Great Britain and said that he hoped that if no further calls were made on his limited training and operational resources one heavy bomber group would be ready in May, a further two in June.

SIR JOHN DILL said that every effort would be made to provide the U.S. Chiefs of Staff with the most up-to-date and realistic picture of the British aircraft position.

AIR MARSHAL EVILL said that he realized the difficulties which the U.S. Chiefs of Staff had found in interpreting certain of the figures which were available and he had asked London to produce at the earliest possible date realistic and practical information which would help the Chiefs of Staff to decide on the future allocation of the available aircraft.

THE COMMITTEE:-

Took note that the Representatives of the British Chiefs of Staff would provide the information needed by the Combined Chiefs of Staff to enable them to allocate available aircraft to the various theaters of war.

U. S. SECRET
BRITISH MOST SECRET

C.C.S. 15th Meeting.

COMBINED CHIEFS OF STAFF

MINUTES of meeting held in Room 240, Combined Chiefs of Staff Building, on Tuesday, April 7, 1942, at 2:30 p.m.

PRESENT

Admiral E. J. King, USN	Field Marshal Sir John Dill
Lt. Gen. H.H. Arnold, USA	Admiral Sir Charles Little
Maj. Gen. G.T. McNarney, USA	Air Marshal D.C.S. Evill
(Representing General Marshall)	Major General R.H. Dewing

THE FOLLOWING WERE ALSO PRESENT

Vice Admiral F. J. Horne, USN	Air Commodore S.C. Strafford
Vice Admiral R. Willson, USN	
Rear Admiral J.H. Towers, USN	
Rear Admiral R.K. Turner, USN	
Brig. Gen. T. T. Handy, USA	
Captain Oscar Smith, USN	
Captain B. H. Bieri, USN	
Commander R. E. Libby, USN	
Lt. Col. H. S. Hansell, USA	
Lt. Col. J. C. Holmes, USA	

ABSENT

General G. C. Marshall, USA

SECRETARIAT

Brigadier V. Dykes
Brig. Gen. W.B. Smith, USA
Commander L.R. McDowell, USN
Commander R.D. Coleridge, RN

U. S. SECRET
BRITISH MOST SECRET

1. GERMAN CAPABILITIES IN TURKEY, SYRIA AND IRAQ.
   (C.C.S. 59)

ADMIRAL KING said that in considering C.C.S. 59 at their meeting on the previous day, the United States Chiefs of Staff had felt that certain information essential to considering the world situation was still lacking. The situation with respect to aircraft, for example, was not sufficiently clear to permit a decision to be made as to whether or not five additional U.S. groups should be sent to the Middle East at the expense of reducing aircraft strength in other areas.

SIR JOHN DILL said that the paper under consideration could be considerably improved and brought up to date by the insertion of figures recently received of strengths of forces now available.

THE COMMITTEE:-

Took note of C.C.S. 59 and directed the Secretaries to refer this paper back to the Combined Intelligence Committee to be brought up to date in the light of the latest information which has become available since the paper was prepared, and to include the German strengths available.

2. UNITED STATES--BRITISH STRATEGY.

Referring to ADMIRAL KING'S request for additional information on which to base strategic allocation of forces, SIR JOHN DILL said that he felt that it was necessary that the Combined Staff Planners should, as a matter of urgency, produce an agreed strategic policy for the United Nations. Such an appreciation would serve as a much needed guide for the allocation of forces, for production of munitions and ships, and the expansion of armed forces necessary for the final offensive.

In the course of discussion it was pointed out that the Combined Staff Planners had already received a directive* instructing them

* C.C.S. 4th Meeting Item 6

U. S. SECRET
BRITISH MOST SECRET

to prepare an appreciation covering the employment of forces in the war against Japan. It was generally agreed that this directive should be widened to include the whole world situation.

SIR JOHN DILL said that an appreciation had been prepared by the British which would be available as a basis for discussion. He hoped that the United States would have a corresponding paper which could be similarly used.

THE COMMITTEE:-

Directed the Combined Staff Planners to prepare an over-all general appreciation leading up to an agreed strategic policy for the United Nations, which will cover major deployment of forces and courses of action for 1942, and intentions for 1943.

3. AIRCRAFT SITUATION OF THE UNITED NATIONS.

With regard to the appreciation referred to in Item 2 above, ADMIRAL KING said that he felt that the difficulties with regard to the allocation of aircraft necessitated an immediate review of the present aircraft resources of the United Nations, together with the proposed expansion programs.

GENERAL ARNOLD agreed with this view. The points which required clarification were the present strength of air forces, the proposed expansions, the present and proposed production programs and the missions to be performed by the aircraft of the United Nations in the various theaters of war.

GENERAL ARNOLD said that he was appreciative of the amount of information which Air Marshal Evill had already provided him with, but the necessity for a combined review of the aircraft situation was emphasized by the continual requests he was receiving to allocate aircraft to individual theaters which, without the full picture, was an impossible task.

U. S. SECRET
BRITISH MOST SECRET

      SIR JOHN DILL welcomed the investigation on the lines suggested by General Arnold. The British aircraft figures would be completely at the disposal of the United States Chiefs of Staff.

      ADMIRAL KING suggested that in order to speed up the procedure, the review of the aircraft situation should be undertaken by General Arnold, Admiral Towers and Air Marshal Evill and when completed this appreciation would fit in to the wider appreciation being undertaken by the Combined Staff Planners.

      GENERAL ARNOLD agreed that sufficient information regarding British aircraft resources was available to enable the study suggested by Admiral King to be undertaken.

      THE COMMITTEE:-

Invited General Arnold, Air Marshal Evill and Admiral Towers to draw up over-all data which will present a complete agreed picture of all U.S. and British air resources to include:

    (a)   Operating strengths

    (b)   Reserves of all types

    (c)   Production

    (d)   Proposed expansion

    (e)   Present distribution by theaters including movements already in progress or arranged.

4.   U.S. AIRCRAFT ALLOCATED TO THE NETHERLANDS EAST INDIES.
      (C.C.S. 60)

      SIR JOHN DILL said that he realized that the Dutch aircraft in question presented a special case and that it therefore might be necessary to depart from the agreed principle that all aircraft should be

U. S. SECRET
BRITISH MOST SECRET

within a common pool from which they would be allocated by the Combined Chiefs of Staff in accordance with strategical needs.

ADMIRAL KING said that as he saw it in this case the U.S. Chiefs of Staff would be acting as the agents of the Combined Chiefs of Staff and the allocation of the Dutch aircraft to the Pacific Theater would be taken into account when considering the needs for aircraft in that theater against the needs of the other theaters.

GENERAL ARNOLD explained that the Netherlands Government had explicitly requested that the United States should take over these aircraft and that they should replace them for use by Dutch pilots at such time as sufficient numbers of these were trained to operate the aircraft. If all these 500 aircraft were put into Australia, the United States would find themselves expected to allocate some 135 aircraft a month in the form of replacements. Certain of these Dutch aircraft were, in fact, scheduled to be sent to India.

THE COMMITTEE:-

(a) Agreed that the U.S. Chiefs of Staff, as agents of the Combined Chiefs of Staff, will make arrangements to take over the Dutch planes as they are produced, including arrangements with the Netherlands Government for their eventual replacement.

(b) Agreed that allocation of these planes should be considered along with the general allocation of aircraft materiel.

(c) Invited General Arnold to draft a note of information on the above to the Australian representatives in Washington, to include particulars of the Dutch aircraft which were being despatched to the Southwest Pacific Area.

U. S. SECRET
BRITISH MOST SECRET

5. PROVISION OF FIGHTER AIRCRAFT FOR AUSTRALIA.
(C.C.S. 30/2)

SIR JOHN DILL explained that the position in the Middle East was such that the British Chiefs of Staff felt it essential that 80 Kittyhawks promised to Australia should be retained in the Middle East but they were anxious not to take unilateral action without the approval of the U.S. Chiefs of Staff.

AIR MARSHAL EVILL pointed out that these 80 aircraft were over and above 125 which had already been specially diverted from the Middle East. This addition was made at a time when the Japanese threat towards Australia seemed more imminent than against India.

In the course of a discussion on the strength of the air forces required in Australia, GENERAL ARNOLD explained that the United States had originally allocated 4 groups (320 operational fighters) to the Southwest Pacific Area. One group had been turned over to the R.A.A.F., and one group diverted to India. He asked whether the Australians would now ask for an additional 80 aircraft from U.S. sources or whether the pursuit group turned over by General Brett to the R.A.A.F. would meet this demand.

AIR MARSHAL EVILL said that it was difficult to assess the number of additional fighters required in Australia pending a decision as to how many of the Dutch fighters would be allocated to the area.

GENERAL ARNOLD agreed to inform Air Marshal Evill of the numbers when a decision had been reached.

ADMIRAL KING pointed out that this problem emphasized the necessity for a very early appreciation of the aircraft resources of the United Nations.

THE COMMITTEE:-

(a) Took note that the U.S. Chiefs of Staff support the

U. S. SECRET
BRITISH MOST SECRET

        British Chiefs of Staff in the retention in the Middle East of eighty fighter aircraft provisionally earmarked for diversion from that theater to Australia.

   (b)   Took note that General Arnold would let Air Marshal Evill have a copy of his note to the Australian representative in Washington (vide conclusion item 4 (c) for the information of the British Chiefs of Staff.

6.   REQUEST FOR AIRCRAFT FROM INDIA.

ADMIRAL KING read out to the Committee a despatch from Colonel Louis Johnson to the President containing a letter from General Wavell to himself on the subject of India's need for aircraft. General Wavell's specific requests were for 40 transport aircraft, 80 reconnaissance aircraft, 120 medium bombers and 120 fighters. With these, in addition to British and U.S. aircraft already allocated to the area, he felt confident of holding India.

With regard to transport aircraft, GENERAL ARNOLD said that within the next 1½ to 2 months there would be 100 U.S. transport aircraft between Suez and Calcutta.

SIR JOHN DILL said that the request should more properly have been put to the British Chiefs of Staff and asked that he might have a copy of the despatch to send to London.

ADMIRAL KING agreed to furnish Sir John Dill with a copy of Colonel Louis Johnson's despatch to the President.

7.   PRODUCTION OF LANDING CRAFT.

ADMIRAL KING said that in the course of discussion at the White House it had been felt that there might be an opportunity to launch an offensive in the autumn of 1942 but that the limiting factor for such

U. S. SECRET
BRITISH MOST SECRET

an offensive might be the availability of landing craft. He had therefore examined the possibilities of increasing the production of landing craft. Improvement in the production of certain types was impossible but the production of tank lighters and landing boats could be improved. He had already given orders that the greatest possible numbers of these craft should be built ready for use by September, 1942. Delays in the completion of certain combatant ships might be incurred but it was thought that only small mine sweepers and some of the larger long-dated combat vessels would be affected.

ADMIRAL KING said that the problem of the transportation of these craft across the Atlantic had not yet been fully investigated but that they would of course be available in the common pool for use by troops of any of the United Nations. If they were not required on the continent in the autumn of 1942 there would be many other uses to which they might be put.

U. S. SECRET
BRITISH MOST SECRET

C.C.S. 16th Meeting

COMBINED CHIEFS OF STAFF

MINUTES of meeting held in Room 240, Combined Chiefs of Staff Building, on Tuesday, April 21, 1942, at 2:30 p.m.

PRESENT

General G. C. Marshall, USA
Admiral E. J. King, USN
Lt. Gen. H. H. Arnold, USA

Sir Dudley Pound, Admiral of the Fleet
Field Marshal Sir John Dill
Air Marshal D.C.S. Evill
Major General R. H. Dewing

THE FOLLOWING WERE ALSO PRESENT

Admiral H. R. Stark, USN
Vice Admiral F.J. Horne, USN
Vice Admiral R. Willson, USN
Rear Admiral J.H. Towers, USN
Rear Admiral R.K. Turner, USN
Maj. Gen. J.T. McNarney, USA
Brig. Gen. H.J. Malony, USA
Brig. Gen. T.T. Handy, USA
Captain Oscar Smith, USN
Captain C. M. Cooke, Jr., USN
Commander R. E. Libby, USN
Commander C. F. Espe, USN
Lt. Col. J. C. Holmes, USA

Admiral Sir Charles Little

SECRETARIAT

Brigadier V. Dykes
Brig. Gen. W.B. Smith, USA
Commander L.R. McDowell, USN
Commander R.D. Coleridge, RN

U. S. SECRET
BRITISH MOST SECRET

1. NAVAL BASES AND REPAIR FACILITIES.
   (C.C.S. 63)

   THE COMMITTEE:-

   (a) Approved the recommendations of the Combined Staff Planners contained in paragraphs 9 to 11 and the priority list proposed in paragraph 12 of C.C.S. 63.

   (b) Directed the Combined Munitions Assignments Board to consider allocations of materiel for LION and CUB bases in the light of current requirements for active projects.

2. RAPID MILITARY COMMUNICATIONS OF THE UNITED NATIONS.
   (C.C.S. 64)

   GENERAL MARSHALL said that the U.S. Chiefs of Staff suggested that the Washington Communications Board should be instructed to review the adequacy of combined communications system for universal application.

   THE COMMITTEE:-

   (a) Approved the draft directive to the Washington Communications Board and the London Communications Committee submitted by the Combined Staff Planners (C.C.S. 64)

   (b) Took note that the U.S. Chiefs of Staff had directed the Washington Communications Board to submit a report by May 15, 1942, of the adequacy of the combined communications system for universal application.

3. ALLOCATION OF TRANSPORT AIRPLANES FOR U.S.S.R.
   (C.C.S. 65)

   THE COMMITTEE had before them a memorandum by the Joint U.S.

U. S. SECRET
BRITISH MOST SECRET

Chiefs of Staff suggesting that the allocation of 29 heavy transport aircraft to Russia made by the Combined Munitions Assignments Board should be disapproved by the Combined Chiefs of Staff.

GENERAL ARNOLD explained that at present only 50 heavy transport aircraft were available in the United States, of which only 10 could be spared for the training of parachute troops. It was therefore necessary to weigh up the relative importance of this diversion to Russia against the impossibility of meeting U.S. commitments for a continental offensive in Europe if this demand were met.

GENERAL MALONY said that in November the Russians had asked for 600 transport aircraft. This demand had been reduced to 400. Later the Russians had asked for 100 transport aircraft at once plus an allocation of 25 a month.

The Munitions Assignments Board (Air) Committee in considering this request felt that on military grounds no transport aircraft should be allocated to Russia but if necessary for political reasons the maximum allocated should be 162. The figure of 29 would be the May and June allocations, further allocations being considered in the light of the new Russian Protocol.

GENERAL ARNOLD stressed the importance of retaining heavy transport aircraft in the United States if the necessary airborne troops for continental operations in the autumn were to be trained. The figures of 200 transport aircraft in August and 400 transport aircraft in November, given in paragraph (c) of C.C.S. 65, would all be available for use from Great Britain. If it were decided to send any of these aircraft to Russia, they could be flown across Africa and in through Basra.

ADMIRAL TOWERS stressed the importance of making at least a small allocation to Russia in view of the political considerations. If this course were decided on, the Navy would be prepared to release a proportion of the aircraft required. He estimated the total production of heavy transport aircraft for the next two months to be 150.

U. S. SECRET
BRITISH MOST SECRET

Both SIR JOHN DILL and AIR MARSHAL EVILL stressed the urgent need of India for transport planes. The Air Ministry had asked for the release of 40 in view of the fact that troops operating in Burma could be supplied only by air. This request was similar to that put forward by Colonel Louis Johnson.

SIR JOHN DILL said that if it were agreed that no transport aircraft could be allocated to Russia then it would be necessary to give a very well reasoned explanation of the present shortage of transport aircraft, including the urgent needs for such types in India and Burma.

SIR JOHN DILL further suggested the possibility of using certain of the older civil airlines' aircraft for the training of airborne troops.

GENERAL ARNOLD said that 80 civil airliners were already in use by the Army, although still run and operated by the civil airlines, and he felt that no further aircraft could be taken from this source. The total number of civil airliners operating in the United States was approximately 330, of which the 80 he had referred to were no longer available for civilian passengers.

GENERAL MARSHALL explained the proposed expansion program for the U.S. airborne troops. The next three months were the critical ones, and it was essential not to cut down training facilities. During his visit to England he had seen exercises carried out by British airborne formations and the number of aircraft available for this important form of training (17) was hopelessly inadequate.

In discussion on continental operations in London, the British Chiefs of Staff had suggested that U.S. parachute troops, together with their aircraft, should be sent over to take part in some of the Commando raids and further that a month before any major operation on the continent it would be necessary to requisition all civil airliners in the United States for use in the operation. He had undertaken to look into this suggestion.

U. S. SECRET
BRITISH MOST SECRET

He agreed with Sir John Dill that in replying to the Russians a very carefully phrased reply would have to be made. He felt that the operational effect of such a small number of aircraft in Russia would be small although the political effect might be considerable, and he realized that Russians in this country resented the large civil air services still running.

GENERAL ARNOLD said that his figures for production of heavy air transport planes were 69 for April and 84 for May. He suggested that the lighter types of air transport planes might be sent to Russia.

AIR MARSHAL EVILL pointed out that this would seriously handicap the British who at present were receiving no allocations of the heavier types but could be using the lighter types very considerably for air transport in the Middle East. He suggested that a balance sheet of transport aircraft should be drawn up showing present and future commitments on the one hand and available aircraft including airliners and production on the other.

THE COMMITTEE:-

(a) Agreed that on strategical grounds the allocation of 29 C-47 and C-53 transport aircraft to Russia during May and June, 1942, should be countermanded.

(b) Instructed the Secretaries to draft, for their approval, a memorandum setting out the strategical considerations which prompted the above decision.

4. USE OF U.S. AIRCRAFT CARRIERS.

SIR JOHN DILL on behalf of the British Chiefs of Staff thanked the U.S. Chiefs of Staff for the use of certain U.S. aircraft carriers.

5. SUPPLIES TO RUSSIA.

SIR DUDLEY POUND outlined the difficulties which were being

U. S. SECRET
BRITISH MOST SECRET

experienced in the supply of weapons to Russia by the northern route. To date this problem had been treated on the basis of availability of supplies and shipping. The basing of Fokke Wulfs, long range bombers, and submarines in Norway, together with surface craft in Trondheim, had seriously increased the difficulties of achieving the safe and timely arrival of convoys from the United Kingdom and the United States. In addition, the ice conditions this year were the worst for some 25 years and some 65 merchant ships were expected to be waiting in Iceland for the next convoy to be put through. Heavy losses must be expected in these convoys.

6. SITUATION IN THE INDIAN OCEAN.

SIR DUDLEY POUND outlined the recent naval and air operations in the Indian Ocean and pointed out the inadequate A.A. defenses of Colombo, Trincomalee and Addu Attol.

He stressed the importance of the control of the Western Indian Ocean which, if lost, would result in the Japanese not only cutting our lines of communications to India and the Middle East, but also stopping oil supplies from the Persian Gulf. If this source of supply were cut, the tanker tonnage available would not be sufficient to supply the area from America.

7. GENERAL MARSHALL'S VISIT TO LONDON.

GENERAL MARSHALL outlined the discussions which took place during his visit to London. He had found the views of the British Chiefs of Staff were almost in complete accord with his own, regarding operations proposed for 1943. One of the points which had been considered was the availability of landing craft for continental operations and he was now investigating the possibility of requisitioning marine engines and outboard motors in the United States. In discussion with the Prime Minister on the degree of publicity already afforded to possible operations on the continent, it had been felt that it might be desirable to issue some carefully phrased communique on the subject.

U. S. SECRET
BRITISH MOST SECRET

8. REVIEW OF THE SITUATION BY ADMIRAL STARK.

In reply to a request, ADMIRAL STARK outlined his views on the present situation. He regarded the Russian army as our most valuable immediate asset and felt we must make every effort to guard against its defeat, which would be a catastrophe of the first magnitude.

With regard to the Middle East, ADMIRAL STARK said that he had always stressed the importance of this theater. If it fell, the blockade of Germany would be broken and it was, in addition, the one place, other than Russia, where a German army was being actively engaged. All operations by the United Nations were dependent on shipping. In a recent conversation with Admiral Land, he had understood that the building of shipping in the United States might be increased from 15 to 35 per cent, if certain labor troubles could be overcome.

With regard to the Pacific our policy should be to stand on the defensive in that area. He deplored the excessive publicity given to this theater in the newspapers.

U. S. SECRET
BRITISH MOST SECRET

C.C.S. 17th Meeting

COMBINED CHIEFS OF STAFF

MINUTES of meeting held in Room 240, Combined Chiefs of Staff Building, on Tuesday, April 28, 1942, at 2:30 p.m.

PRESENT

General G. C. Marshall, USA
Lt. General H. H. Arnold, USA
Vice Admiral F. J. Horne, USN
(Representing Admiral King)

Field Marshal Sir John Dill
Admiral Sir Charles Little
Air Marshal D.C.S. Evill
Major General R. H. Dewing

THE FOLLOWING WERE ALSO PRESENT

Vice Admiral R. Willson, USN
Rear Admiral J.H. Towers, USN
Rear Admiral R.K. Turner, USN
Maj. Gen. J. T. McNarney, USA
Brig. Gen. H. J. Malony, USA
Brig. Gen. T. T. Handy, USA
Captain Oscar Smith, USN
Captain C. M. Cooke, Jr., USN
Commander R. E. Libby, USN
Commander C. F. Espe, USN
Lt. Col. J. C. Holmes, USA

Captain G. D. Belben, RN
Captain J. A. Grindle, RN
Brigadier G. K. Bourne
Air Cdr. S. C. Strafford

ABSENT

Admiral E.J. King, USN

SECRETARIAT

Brigadier V. Dykes
Brig. Gen. W.B. Smith, USA
Commander L.R. McDowell, USN

U. S. SECRET
BRITISH MOST SECRET

1.   TRANSPORT AIRCRAFT FOR BURMA AND INDIA.
          (C.C.S. 52/1 - C.C.S. 52/2)

SIR JOHN DILL stressed the urgent necessity for increase of transport aircraft in India and Burma. He considered the general situation in that area to be deteriorating and stated that there were only four transport aircraft in Burma and twenty-four in India. The forty additional requested from the United States would not be used on a steady run, but as a mobile force available wherever their services would be of greatest assistance.

GENERAL ARNOLD said that consideration was now being given as to the best use of all available transport aircraft and cited figures on the current situation regarding these planes. First priority of allocation was given those planes assigned to England for use of airborne and parachute troops and glider operations, for which purpose he expected there would be sent 200 by August and a further 200 by October. The second priority was given to the Air Ferry Command which now had 57 planes and which, it was contemplated, would be built up to a total of 284 by December. Thirty-four planes were now en route to the Burma-China theater as part of a total of 75 which were committed there. The next priority was given to the planes for the Karachi-Calcutta area, which he hoped soon to build up to a total of 40 planes. He further hoped to build up the trans-African Ferry Service to a total of 40 about the same time. When all present commitments were made and a small number retained in the United States, the estimated U.S. requirements would lack about 369 planes. In view of the above, he considered that reductions must be made somewhere, and that the best use which could be made of available planes would be to operate them in such a way that they could be sent to any area where their services were most needed.

SIR JOHN DILL considered that a better or greater mobility of air transport would be possible if certain of the planes in India were under the control of the British Commander in Chief.

GENERAL MARSHALL appreciated the desire of the Commander in Chief to have some aircraft on the use of which he could rely. It was to

U. S. SECRET
BRITISH MOST SECRET

help in this respect that General Brereton had been ordered to operate under the orders of the British.

GENERAL ARNOLD mentioned the three types of transport service now in being in India:

(a) A special service from the U.S. to India and China, returning to the U.S. via India, which used very few planes. All of these were controlled directly from the United States.

(b) Transport planes destined for China, of which there were now 44, with expectation of an increase to a total of 75 by this summer. These were under the direction of General Stilwell.

(c) The trans-India service, where he expected to have 20 in May and 40 in the late summer, under direct control of General Brereton.

In replying to a question by General Marshall, AIR MARSHAL EVILL said that there were 431 transport planes allocated for delivery to England this year. Seventy small transport planes (C-61) had been allocated, but no large transports (C-47 and C-53) would be delivered until after mid-summer. These latter, he feared, would arrive too late for service in India. He considered that at the present time suitable air transport service in India would be invaluable to the Army and would double the value of the air units, while planes delivered two months hence would arrive too late to do much good.

THE COMMITTEE:-

Took note that General Marshall would examine the situation further to determine if any action can be taken, either by specific directive to General Brereton or otherwise, to ameliorate the acute situation with respect to air transport in Burma and India.

U. S. SECRET
BRITISH MOST SECRET

2. AUXILIARY AIRCRAFT CARRIERS.
   (C.C.S. 62/1)

ADMIRAL HORNE mentioned that arrangements had been made for the production of 24 C-3 type hulls to be converted into auxiliary aircraft carriers each year as long as they were required.

THE COMMITTEE:-

   (a) Agreed to approve the recommendations contained in the basic paper.

   (b) Directed the Secretaries to inform the Munitions Assignments Board of this decision.

3. TRANSPORT OF SMALL NUMBERS OF TROOPS ON CARGO VESSELS TO BRITAIN FROM NORTH AMERICA.
   (C.C.S. 66)

In the brief discussion of this subject, SIR JOHN DILL mentioned that the British policy was not to transport additional personnel on cargo vessels which had a speed of less than 12 knots, inasmuch as it was considered too dangerous for ships carrying men if for any reason they fell behind the convoy and were unable to rejoin.

THE COMMITTEE:-

Took note of the report and approved the recommendations of the Combined Military Transportation Committee.

4. PREPARATION OF WAR PLAN BOLERO.
   (C.P.S. 26/2/D)

SIR JOHN DILL inquired as to when the U.S. would send a planning team to the U.K.

GENERAL MARSHALL said that in addition to an officer from the Operations and Plans Division for the London Committee, two officers, one

U. S. SECRET
BRITISH MOST SECRET

logistics expert and one planning expert, were leaving to join the staff of General Paget, while three officers from the Army and some from the Navy were soon to join Combined Operations Headquarters. He also had in mind sending to England a corps commander with his staff.

Some discussion followed on the procedure to be adopted by the two committees in Washington and London. It was generally agreed that the London Committee would deal primarily with questions of port capacity and accommodation, while the Washington Committee would be principally concerned with production questions. A troop movement program would have to be drawn up by the two Committees working in the closest cooperation.

SIR JOHN DILL considered that the provision of landing craft was the governing factor in the proposed operations and inquired whether production of these craft could in any way be speeded up, particularly the large tank landing ships.

ADMIRAL HORNE, in reply, said that a new program of landing craft production would shortly be ready. In August, some 250 landing craft would be available for use in England. Of these, 23 had already been shipped, 53 were in New York awaiting shipment, while an additional 40 would be ready in less than a week. He added that every effort was being made to speed up production of the 2,300 landing craft of various types now proposed for the operation.

ADMIRAL LITTLE suggested the advisability of broadening the terms of the directive to the Combined Staff Planners to include an account of all landing craft which would be available in the U.K. by April 1943.

ADMIRAL TURNER stated that this was envisaged, in that the Combined Staff Planners would be able to state how many craft would be available by August 15, 1942, and by April 1, 1943.

THE COMMITTEE:-

    (a) Took note of the arrangements made to send U.S. staff personnel to London.

U. S. SECRET
BRITISH MOST SECRET

        (b) Took note that the Landing Craft Committee would include in their report a forecast of all landing craft of U.K. and U.S. production which would be available for operations from the United Kingdom by
            (1) August 15, 1942
            (2) April 1, 1943

        (c) Took note that the U.S. planes scheduled to go to the United Kingdom in May would all be ready prior to June 1. The Senior Headquarters have already left U.S. Transportation of manpower, bombs and organizational equipment depends on available water transport.

5.   DIRECTIVE FOR ASSIGNMENT OF MUNITIONS.
       (C.C.S. 50/2 (appendices))

    SIR JOHN DILL, considering that allocations of aircraft under the Arnold-Portal agreement were well understood, suggested that this agreement be continued as a basis for allocations until such time as the report of the Arnold-Evill-Towers Committee had been approved. Confusion was likely to be caused by adopting a new basis for a short time which would probably be subject to considerable change upon completion of the Committee's report.

    ADMIRAL TURNER spoke in favor of the system of priorities for the allocation of aircraft contained in the appendices under discussion, on the ground that this allocation was based on strategic considerations and the allocations were by theaters, whereas the Arnold-Portal agreement merely assigned planes without regard to strategic priority. He added that the Munitions Assignments Board was most desirous of having their directive completed by receipt of these appendices. While it was fully realized that the figures therein were tentative and would change somewhat upon completion of a study now being made along broad strategical lines, the Munitions Assignments Board could use the figures for at least the next few months while taking into consideration the likelihood of future changes.

U. S. SECRET
BRITISH MOST SECRET

AIR MARSHAL EVILL, agreeing with Sir John Dill, stressed the desirability of continuing assignments on the present basis rather than to introduce a policy of assignments admittedly temporary.

GENERAL MALONY considered that the subject was one of greater scope than mere assignment, in that strategic dispositions adopted would influence the production schedules.

THE COMMITTEE:-

Accepted the appendices and directed the Secretaries to transmit them to the Munitions Assignments Board for use in conjunction with the assignments directive (C.C.S. 50/2) subject to the proviso that the Arnold-Portal Agreement should remain the basis for aircraft assignments pending the adoption by the Combined Chiefs of Staff of a new basis resulting from the report of the Arnold-Evill-Towers Committee.

6. REQUISITION OF MATERIEL FOR THE SOUTHWEST PACIFIC AREA.
   (C.C.S. 68)

GENERAL MALONY described two proposals for dealing with allocations to Australia which had been discussed by the London Munitions Assignments Board. These were, in brief, as follows:

(a) (1) Australian army and air requirements should be dealt with in Washington.

    (2) Australian naval requirements, with certain exceptions, should be dealt with in London.

If the above conclusions were accepted, it was proposed that Australian requirements for small arms ammunition also be dealt with in Washington, since the Army and Air Force are the major users.

(b) (1) Australian air requirements to be dealt with in Washington.

U. S. SECRET
BRITISH MOST SECRET

        (2)   Australian naval and army requirements, with certain exceptions, to be dealt with in London.

If accepted, small arms ammunition would also be dealt with in London as at present.

The representatives of the British Chiefs of Staff stated that they were not prepared to discuss this matter and requested a deferment until the next meeting.

GENERAL SMITH informed the Committee that Dr. Evatt had given his approval to the methods of requisitioning set forth in C.C.S. 68.

THE COMMITTEE:-

Agreed to defer consideration, pending further study by the representatives of the British Chiefs of Staff.

7.   VICHY FRANCE POSSESSIONS IN THE CARIBBEAN.

ADMIRAL HORNE, in reply to a question by Sir John Dill, described certain proposals regarding the Vichy France possessions in the Caribbean.

U. S. SECRET
BRITISH MOST SECRET

C.C.S. 18th Meeting

COMBINED CHIEFS OF STAFF

MINUTES of meeting held in Room 240,
Combined Chiefs of Staff Building, on Tuesday, May
5, 1942, at 2:30 p.m.

PRESENT

General G. C. Marshall, USA	Field Marshal Sir John Dill
Admiral E. J. King, USN	Admiral Sir Charles Little
Lt. Gen. H. H. Arnold, USA	Air Marshal D.C.S. Evill
	Major General R.H. Dewing

THE FOLLOWING WERE ALSO PRESENT

Vice Admiral F. J. Horne, USN	Lt. General E. K. Smart (For Item 1)
Vice Admiral R. Willson, USN	Air Cdr. S. C. Strafford
Rear Admiral J. H. Towers, USN	
Rear Admiral R. K. Turner, USN	
Maj. Gen. J. T. McNarney, USA	
Maj. Gen. D.D. Eisenhower, USA	
Brig. Gen. H. J. Malony, USA	
Brig. Gen. T. T. Handy, USA	
Captain Oscar Smith, USN	
Captain C. M. Cooke, Jr., USN	
Commander R. E. Libby, USN	
Commander C. F. Espe, USN	
Lt. Col. J. C. Holmes, USA	

SECRETARIAT

Brigadier V. Dykes
Brig. Gen. W.B. Smith, USA
Commander L.R. McDowell, USN
Commander R.D. Coleridge, RN

U. S. SECRET
BRITISH MOST SECRET

1. REQUISITION OF MATERIAL FOR SOUTHWEST PACIFIC AREA.
   (C.C.S. 68)

SIR JOHN DILL said that while the principle of General MacArthur approving all requisitions from the theater would be acceptable to the British Chiefs of Staff, it would be necessary to obtain the Australian Government's consent. He hoped that the full details of the proposal would be explained to them. Discussions were now in progress with Australia as to whether Australian ground requirements as well as air requirements should be dealt with in Washington. Their naval requirement would presumably continue to be sent to London.

GENERAL SMART said that as the Southwest Pacific was an area of United States responsibility it seemed right that all demands from that area should be initiated by General MacArthur. Dr. Evatt was now in London where he was presumably discussing the matter and he felt it wise to await the views of the Australian Government.

ADMIRAL KING said that it seemed logical that all demands from the Southwest Pacific Area should be correlated in Washington to avoid duplication.

THE COMMITTEE:-

Agreed to defer further consideration of this matter pending the receipt of the Australian Government's views.

2. TRANSPORT AIRCRAFT FOR INDIA.
   (C.C.S. 52/2, Previous References: C.C.S. 9th Meeting, Minute 4, C.C.S 15th Meeting, Minute 6)

GENERAL ARNOLD outlined the present position with regard to transport aircraft in India, Burma and China. General Stilwell had a total of 16 aircraft, 6 operating under C.N.A.C. and 10 under his own control. Nineteen aircraft were en route to him and 23 more were about to leave the United States. The Japanese northern advance, including the capture of the aerodromes at Lashio and Mandalay, had put the Japanese

U. S. SECRET
BRITISH MOST SECRET

within 200 miles of the main airport on the alternate route to China which they could now interrupt. This would entail the use of the direct route which led over 13,000 foot mountains and therefore severely limited the load which could be carried from India into China. General Brereton had at present 4 transport aircraft with one further aircraft at Khartoum and 5 en route. He would in addition shortly have 8 which had been loaned to General Stilwell. The total transport aircraft in the area which it was hoped would be achieved by the middle or the latter part of June would be 25 under General Brereton and 40 under General Stilwell. If the route to China were cut, the aircraft under General Stilwell would remain under his control but might be used in India, though it was more likely that they would be used within China.

GENERAL ARNOLD added that he had suggested to Air Marshal Evill that the British might convert certain Lockheed Ventura aircraft now in the United States for use as transports. He had ascertained that the Lockheed firm could complete this alteration in 10 days, making each aircraft capable of transporting 25 men.

AIR MARSHAL EVILL agreed that this solution was a possibility. There were at present approximately 120 Venturas in the United States. This number had accumulated owing partly to lack of certain items of equipment and partly to a holdup in ferrying. However, the aircraft were badly needed by Bomber Command to relieve Bostons of which the British were already short due to diversions to Russia.

SIR JOHN DILL reiterated the urgent need for transport aircraft in India and expressed his disappointment that no more could be made available at present.

3. AIR OFFENSIVE OVER WESTERN EUROPE--REQUIREMENTS OF PURSUIT AIRCRAFT.
(C.C.S. 69)

GENERAL MARSHALL asked that consideration of this paper be deferred.

U. S. SECRET
BRITISH MOST SECRET

AIR MARSHAL EVILL furnished a more detailed statement of the British fighter position in the United Kingdom and agreed to elaborate this statement to General Arnold.

4. SITUATION IN THE PHILIPPINES.

GENERAL MARSHALL read to the Committee two despatches from General Wainwright, the latest of which originated at about midnight, 4/5 May, 1942, reporting that a Japanese landing on the northern part of the island had just begun.

5. ENEMY INTENTIONS.

In reply to a question by General Marshall, SIR JOHN DILL said that he considered the use of gas by the Germans would indicate that they had embarked on a desperate venture. The British population were well protected against this menace but its use by the Japanese in India would have serious consequences. The British would not use gas prior to the initiation of this type of warfare by the enemy but were ready to do so. As a defensive measure the beaches could be soaked in a persistent gas. There were no indications that the Germans had any new type of gas.

GENERAL EISENHOWER outlined a report by Colonel Ratay, **recently** U.S. Military Attache in Bucharest and Lisbon, who had a very thorough knowledge of European military affairs and had predicted the German attack on Russia with extreme accuracy. Colonel Ratay estimated that the strength of the German forces in the spring of 1942 was greater than ever before and that they would have available a total of 40 thousand aircraft of all types. He was convinced that the Germans would attack England this spring. They would not attack either in Russia or the Middle East and would use only from one hundred to one hundred and twenty-five divisions to hold the Russian front. The Germans had trained vast numbers of airborne troops and he estimated that in a maximum of three to five days between two hundred and two hundred and fifty thousand German airborne troops could be landed in England who would concentrate in cells of resistance all over the country. This would be followed by

U. S. SECRET
BRITISH MOST SECRET

a strong air attack and a sea borne landing, the spearhead of which would consist of mechanized troops. The large number of torpedo carrying aircraft now being built in Germany would be used against British shipping and warships.

GENERAL ARNOLD said that while it was estimated that the German aircraft industry could maintain their original front line strength, this strength had in fact appeared, from reports available, to have dwindled and it seemed reasonable therefore to presume that an air force, not now in use, was being built up.

AIR MARSHAL EVILL said that there were clear indications of the training of a large number of glider troops and this form of operation was not easy to deal with.

GENERAL McNARNEY emphasized the danger of German paratroop attacks on British R.D.F. stations, some of which had seemed to him to be insufficiently protected. The loss of R.D.F. stations would very seriously reduce the value of the British fighter command.

GENERAL DEWING outlined the conclusions of the Committee, of which he had been a member, which had considered the possibility of invasion of England from the German point of view. They had no knowledge of the German training in night glider operations, which was a most difficult feat even on a bright moonlight night and was impracticable on a dark night. It had been considered that the most effective attack would be initiated by heavy bombing, the dropping of paratroops for attacking R.D.F. stations and communications, particularly signal communications, and followed up by a seaborne attack. It was estimated at that time that the number of sorties required for all these purposes was larger than could be provided from the resources available to the Germans. The warning of a seaborne attack would be at least one month. It was therefore probable that all preparations would be made and the actual moment of launching then deferred in order that some measure of surprise would be achieved. With regard to gas, it had been felt that, though the Germans would probably make use of it, they would not gain much advantage thereby.

U. S. SECRET
BRITISH MOST SECRET

C.C.S. 19th Meeting

COMBINED CHIEFS OF STAFF

MINUTES of meeting held in Room 240,
Combined Chiefs of Staff Building, on Tuesday, May
12, 1942, at 2:30 p.m.

PRESENT

General G. C. Marshall, USA	Field Marshal Sir John Dill
Admiral E. J. King, USN	Admiral Sir Charles Little
Lt. Gen. H. H. Arnold, USA	Air Marshal D.C.S. Evill
	Major General R. H. Dewing

THE FOLLOWING WERE ALSO PRESENT

Vice Admiral F. J. Horne, USN	Captain J.A. Grindle, RN
Vice Admiral R. Willson, USN	Air Cdr. S. C. Strafford
Rear Admiral J. H. Towers, USN	
Rear Admiral R. K. Turner, USN	
Maj. Gen. J. T. McNarney, USA	
Maj. Gen. D.D. Eisenhower, USA	
Brig. Gen. T. T. Handy, USA	
Captain Oscar Smith, USN	
Captain C. M. Cooke, Jr., USN	
Commander R. E. Libby, USN	
Commander C. F. Espe, USN	
Lt. Col. J. C. Holmes, USA	

SECRETARIAT

Brigadier V. Dykes
Brig. Gen. W.B. Smith, USA
Commander L.R. McDowell, USN
Commander R.D. Coleridge, RN

U. S. SECRET
BRITISH MOST SECRET

1. AIR OFFENSIVE OVER WESTERN EUROPE-REQUIREMENTS OF PURSUIT AIRCRAFT.
   (C.C.S. 69, Previous Reference: C.C.S. 18th Meeting, Item 3)

   At the suggestion of GENERAL MARSHALL,

   THE COMMITTEE:-

   Agreed that the problem contained in C.C.S. 69 should be studied by the Arnold-Evill-Towers Committee as part of the overall consideration of the allocation of the aircraft of the United Nations, now being undertaken by this body.

2. NAVAL BASES--PLANNING, OPERATION AND PROVISION OF PERSONNEL AND MATERIALS.
   (C.C.S. 67)

   GENERAL MARSHALL suggested that where reference was made to the Governments concerned this should be altered to read "The Chiefs of Staff of the Power concerned," thus bringing the subject, which was essentially military in nature, on to the Chiefs of Staff and not the political level.

   ADMIRAL LITTLE stated that London had agreed with the terms of the document but had suggested that the concurrence of Australia and New Zealand should be sought. This was being done.

   THE COMMITTEE:-

   (a) Approved the re-draft of C.C.S. 67 as presented by General Marshall; and

   (b) Instructed the Secretaries to issue this re-draft as a Combined Chiefs of Staff Directive on receipt of the formal concurrence of the Australian and New Zealand Chiefs of Staff.

U. S. SECRET
BRITISH MOST SECRET

3. REQUISITION OF MATERIAL FOR THE SOUTHWEST PACIFIC AREA.
(C.C.S. 68)

The Committee was informed that a Supply Council had been set up in Australia of which either General MacArthur or a member of his staff would be a member, and that Australia had agreed that all requisitions from the Southwest Pacific Area should be approved by General MacArthur before forwarding to either London or Washington.

GENERAL MARSHALL stated that the object was to expedite the flow of supplies to Australia and suggested that General MacArthur, in consultation with the Australian Supply Council, should be asked to put forward proposals for the necessary machinery for requisitioning material for the area. On receipt of these proposals, the Munitions Assignments Board could complete the plans and prepare the Supply Directive for the approval of the Combined Chiefs of Staff.

THE COMMITTEE:-

(a) Took note that the Australian Government had taken action which appeared to be in conformity with the principle that all requisitions from the Southwest Pacific Area should have the approval of the Supreme Commander.

(b) Agreed that on receipt of the proposals of the Australian Government and General MacArthur as to the machinery for presenting these requisitions, the Combined Munitions Assignments Board should prepare the necessary directive for the approval of the Combined Chiefs of Staff.

4. MOVEMENT OF TROOPS FOR BOLERO.

SIR JOHN DILL asked if any decision by the Combined Chiefs of Staff was required to insure the implementation of the plan for the movement of U.S. troops to the United Kingdom.

U. S. SECRET
BRITISH MOST SECRET

ADMIRAL TURNER reported that the Combined Bolero Committee had put forward to the Combined Staff Planners a proposed plan of troop movements. London had been asked at what rate they could accommodate these troops and in what order the ground units should arrive. The problem of escorts for this large troop movement was being studied. It was hoped that 105,000 troops would be in the United Kingdom by September, 1942, and 800,000 by April, 1943. These movements would entail delay in the relief of the 11,000 British troops remaining in Iceland until after September 1, 1942.

GENERAL HANDY said that no decision by the Combined Chiefs of Staff was required at this stage to implement the moves planned to take place in May and June. When the plans mentioned by Admiral Turner had been completed, a report would be put forward to the Combined Chiefs of Staff showing the program of movements.

GENERAL ARNOLD said that it was hoped that there would be 8 U.S. transport groups in the United Kingdom by October, 1942, in addition to 2 heavy bombardment, 2 medium bombardment, and 2 pursuit groups.

THE COMMITTEE:-

 (a) Agreed that troop movements for BOLERO should proceed with all dispatch.

 (b) Took note that the sailings for May and June had already been arranged, and that the preparation of *tentative programs for later movements for which convoy arrangements were still under consideration was being expedited.*

5.   ALLOCATION OF AIRCRAFT OF THE UNITED NATIONS.

GENERAL ARNOLD stated that General Spaatz with his staff would be going to London at the end of this month. The Arnold-Evill-Towers Committee were very conscious of the necessity of arriving at agreed decisions at the earliest possible moment but with regard to the proposed

U. S. SECRET
BRITISH MOST SECRET

visit of the Committee to London there were certain basic decisions which would first have to be reached.

SIR JOHN DILL reminded the Committee of the importance of a speedy decision on the allocation of aircraft, more particularly as the possibility of undertaking operations on the continent in 1942 would depend on these decisions.

U. S. SECRET
BRITISH MOST SECRET

C.C.S. 20th Meeting

COMBINED CHIEFS OF STAFF

MINUTES of meeting held in Room 240, Combined Chiefs of Staff Building, on Tuesday, May 19, 1942, at 2:30 p.m.

PRESENT

General G. C. Marshall, USA
Lt. Gen. H. H. Arnold, USA
Vice Admiral R. Willson, USN
(Representing Adm. King)

Field Marshal Sir John Dill
Admiral Sir Charles Little
Air Marshal D.C.S. Evill
Major General R. H. Dewing

THE FOLLOWING WERE ALSO PRESENT

Vice Admiral F. J. Horne, USN
Rear Admiral J.H. Towers, USN
Rear Admiral R.K. Turner, USN
Maj. Gen. J.T. McNarney, USA
Brig. Gen. H. J. Malony, USA
Brig. Gen. T. T. Handy, USA
Captain Oscar Smith, USN
Captain C. M. Cooke, Jr., USN
Commander R. E. Libby, USN
Commander C. F. Espe, USN
Lt. Col. J. C. Holmes, USA

Brigadier G. K. Bourne

ABSENT

Admiral E. J. King, USN

SECRETARIAT

Brigadier V. Dykes
Brig. Gen. W.B. Smith, USA
Commander L.R. McDowell, USN
Commander R.D. Coleridge, RN

U. S. SECRET
BRITISH MOST SECRET

1. UNITED STATES AIR ATTACK ON JAPAN.

GENERAL MARSHALL gave a brief resume of the very successful air attack carried out on targets in Japan in mid-April.

2. BOLERO.
(C.C.S. 72)

SIR JOHN DILL said that the British Chiefs of Staff were anxious to get the remaining British troops out of Iceland before September when the weather became bad, and in order to complete the divisional formation in England. It was hoped that additional shipping could be found. It would be useful if the Bolero Committee could report to the Combined Chiefs of Staff at regular intervals on the progress of this plan.

THE COMMITTEE:-

(a) Took note that the British Chiefs of Staff wished to have the relief of the British troops in Iceland completed before September, and instructed the Combined Military Transportation Committee, in consultation with the Bolero Combined Committee, to investigate and report on the best method of so doing.

(b) Subject to the above qualification, approved the tentative shipping program for troop movements during July and August and cargo shipments during June, July and August, 1942, as set out in paragraphs 3 and 5 of the Annex to C.C.S. 72.

(c) Instructed the Combined Staff Planners to report progress and future planned movements to the Combined Chiefs of Staff at frequent intervals.

3. ADEQUACY OF COMBINED COMMUNICATIONS.
(C.C.S. 71)

U. S. SECRET
BRITISH MOST SECRET

GENERAL MARSHALL said that the United States Chiefs of Staff felt that the Washington Communications Board should be instructed to submit recommendations for the amendment of its Directive (C.C.S. 64) in order to provide the Board with sufficient executive authority to issue directives on the broad aspects of the technical phases of communications.

The Committee were informed that arrangements had been made for Communication Officers to be available for consultation by the Combined Staff Planners as necessary, though these would not serve as members of the Combined Staff Planners.

THE COMMITTEE:-

    (a) Accepted C.C.S. 71 subject to the deletion of paragraph 5.

    (b) Instructed the Washington Communications Board to submit, for their approval, a revised Directive designed to provide them with sufficient executive authority to implement agreed technical policy without further reference to higher authority.

    (c) Took note that Communications Officers would be available to the Combined Staff Planners for consultation as might be necessary.

4.   GERMAN CAPABILITIES IN SYRIA AND IRAQ.
    (Previous Reference: C.C.S. 15th Meeting, Item 1, C.C.S. 59/1)

GENERAL MARSHALL said that in the opinion of the War Department, German capabilities might have been under-estimated. The length of time before the Germans could advance towards the Persian Gulf from secure Syrian bases was likely to be five months instead of from seven and one-half to nine months as envisaged in the report.

SIR JOHN DILL agreed that the paper under-estimated German capabilities, particularly, he thought, with regard to the time factor

U. S. SECRET
BRITISH MOST SECRET

involved in the capture of Cyprus, and the subsequent attack on Syria.

THE COMMITTEE:-

Accepted the Combined Intelligence Report (C.C.S. 59/1) subject to the provisos mentioned above by General Marshall and Sir John Dill.

5. AIR OFFENSIVE AGAINST ENEMY SUBMARINE BASES, BUILDING YARDS AND HEAVY SHIPS.
   (Memorandum by CinC, U.S. Fleet, and Chief of Naval Operations, C.C.S. 73)

SIR JOHN DILL said that the problem outlined by Admiral King was one which had been receiving the constant consideration of the British Chiefs of Staff since the beginning of the war. The importance of naval targets and particularly submarines had frequently been stressed by the First Sea Lord and the weight of attack on this form of target had been increased from time to time, particularly in the last few months. The submarine menace was very serious and was threatening the maintenance of our vital sea communications. The coastal command of the Royal Air Force had recently been increased to assist in combatting this menace, and raids on such places as Augsburg, where Diesel engines for submarines were being made, had been planned to slow up German submarine production.

SIR JOHN DILL presented a note on the subject of the selection of targets together with tables showing the weight of attack during February, 1942, on various types of targets.

ADMIRAL LITTLE said that it had been hoped to build up the number of escort vessels available to the United Nations to a number whereby as many as 12 to 15 escorts could be provided for each convoy. This would make submarine attacks very difficult and take such a heavy toll that they would not become worthwhile. The losses of boats and trained crews might break the morale of the German submarine personnel. The rate of German building, however, had enabled them to increase the

U. S. SECRET
BRITISH MOST SECRET

area in which attacks could be made and therefore, while more escort vessels were available, the areas over which convoying was essential had increased, thus preventing more escort vessels being available for each convoy.

SIR JOHN DILL said that upon arrival of United States bomber forces in the United Kingdom, it would be necessary to consider the most useful targets for both them and the Royal Air Force to attack. He undertook to refer Admiral King's memorandum to the British Chiefs of Staff.

THE COMMITTEE:-

(a) Invited the Representatives of the British Chiefs of Staff to forward C.C.S. 73 to London requesting an expression of views by the British Chiefs of Staff.

(b) Agreed to defer consideration of the paper pending receipt of these views.

U. S. SECRET
BRITISH MOST SECRET

May 20, 1942.

COMBINED CHIEFS OF STAFF

CORRIGENDUM
to
MINUTES of meeting held on
Tuesday, May 19, 1942.
(20th Meeting)

All holders are requested to add the following new item:

6. NEW TYPE OF GERMAN GAS.
    (Previous reference: C.C.S. 18th Meeting, Item 5)

SIR JOHN DILL said that since discussing the question of new gases at a previous meeting, he had been informed by London that the Germans were now known to possess a new odorless gas, suitable for surprise attack by inclusion in bombardments from the ground or from the air. This gas was known as "Green Ring One" and its effect on the eyes was serious, though its effect on the skin was less than that of mustard gas. Full details of this gas has been given to the U.S. War Department.

V. DYKES

W. B. SMITH

Combined Secretariat.

SUBJECT		PAGE NO.
ABDA AREA:	Additional U.S. Troops For	46
	British Naval Forces In	C.C.S. 10
	Dissolution Of	61-62
	Dutch Take Over Command	62
	General Situation In	43,53,57,70
	General Wavell's Appreciation Of Situation In	2
	Heavy Bomber Squadrons to Burma	53
	Inclusion of Darwin In	16
	Naval Command In	38
	Naval Reinforcements For	3,13,23,48
	New Western Boundary	58,61
	Pacific War Council In London	53
	Relation Between Naval And Air Operations	44
	Supplies For The Dutch In	10,16
	Supplies From Australia	62
	Transfer Of British Submarines From	64
ABDACOM:	Location Of Headquarters In Melbourne	57
AIR:	Offensive Against Enemy Bases, Yards, And Ships	155
	Possibility Of German Offensive Against England	145
AIRCRAFT:	Arnold-Evill-Towers Committee	122
	Arnold-Portal Agreement As Basis For Allocation	139
	Bombardment Groups:	
	Allocation to U.K.	20,50,65
	For Australia (Heavy)	71
	Force For India	65
	Force For Middle East	65
	Burma To Australia, Diversion From	87

I

SUBJECT		PAGE NO.
AIRCRAFT: (Continued)	Cairo, Proposals For U.S. Units In	99
	Carriers, Auxilliary	137
	Civilian Aircraft For Coastal Patrols	94
	Fighter: Additional for N.E.I.	37
	For Australia	124
	For India	124-125
	Movement Of Planes Instead Of Complete Units	94
	N.E.I., Allocated To	114,122
	N.E.I., U.S. Schedule For Delivery To	86
	Pursuit: For Australia and New Zealand	65
	For Middle East	65
	Requirements For European Air Offensive	144,148
	To Accompany Heavy Bombardment Groups to U.K.	50
	U.S. Squadrons to Egypt	64
	Requirements Of All Theaters	66
	Resources, Total British	118
	Resources, United Nations	121
	Shortage Of, Versus Shortage Of Pilots	95
	Transport: Allocation Of For USSR	128
	For Burma And India	72,135,143
	For China	143
	For India, Request For	130
	General Allocations	130
	United Nations, Allocations Of	150
	United Nations, Production Of	37
	U.S. Training	129
	Variety Of Requests For	117
AIR FORCES:	British Request 100 Antisubmarine Bombers	117
	Economical Employment Of Against Japan	37
	Policy For Disposition Of U.S. And British	64
	Reinforcement Of For Middle East	95

II

SUBJECT			PAGE NO.
AIR LINERS, CIVIL:	Use by Army		130
AIR ROUTE:	West African		49
ALEXANDER, General:	Takes Command Of British Forces		86
ANZAC AREA	General Situation In		43
	Governmental And Strategical Control And Commands In		78
	Institution Of		31
	Naval Forces In		13
	U.S. Commander In		4
	U.S. Sphere		44
AREAS:	ABDA:	Additional U.S. Troops For	46
		British Naval Forces In	C.C.S. 10
		Dissolution Of	61-62
		Dutch Take Over Command	62
		General Situation In	43,53,57,70
		General Wavell's Appreciation Of Situation In	2
		Heavy Bomber Squadrons to Burma	53
		Inclusion Of Darwin In	16
		Naval Command In	38
		Naval Reinforcements For	3,13,23,48
		New Western Boundary	58,61
		Pacific War Council in London	53
		Relation Between Naval And Air Operations	44
		Supplies For The Dutch In	10,16
		Supplies From Australia	62
		Transfer Of British Submarines From	64
	ANZAC:	Control and Commands In	87
		General Situation In	43
		Governmental And Strategical Control And Commands In	78
		Institution Of	31
		Naval Forces In	13
		U.S. Commander In	4
		U.S. Sphere	44
	PHILIPPINE:	Supplies For	2,5
	STRATEGIC:	In Japanese War Zone	87
	WESTERN ATLANTIC:	Change In, As Defined in ABC-1	8,40

SUBJECT		PAGE NO.
ARNOLD, General:	Arnold-Evill-Towers Committee	122
	Arnold-Portal Agreement As Basis For Allocations of Aircraft	139
ASCENSION ISLAND:	Terms Of Occupancy	108
AUSTRALIA:	Air Requirements For	36
	Allocation Of Aircraft Purchased By Dutch	114
	Bases Between Hawaii And	44
	British Allocation Of Pursuit Planes	26
	Defense of N.E. Approaches	26
	Fighter Aircraft For	124
	Heavy Bombers For	71
	Japanese Intentions Against	88,92
	Naval Reinforcements For	2
	Possible Japanese Action Against	25
	Proposals Re Sphere of Responsibility	78
	Pursuit Squadrons For	65
	Supplies to ABDA Area	62
	Surplus Of Pilots	95
	Troops For Burma	43
	Troops In Middle East	113
	Views Regarding Strategic Responsibility	112
A.V.G.:	Employment Of In Burma And China	6,18,31
BASES:	Between Hawaii And Australia	44
	LION and CUB	128
	Naval, And Repair Facilities	128
	Naval, In Indian Ocean	77,98
	Naval, Supervision Of	148
	Pacific: Air Forces	35
	Land Forces	36
	Submarine, Proposed Air Offensive	155

SUBJECT		PAGE NO.
BOLERO:	Movement of Troops	149
	Preparation Of War Plan	137
	Program For Troop And Cargo Movement	153
	U.S. Planning Personnel To England	138
BOMBARDMENT GROUPS:	Allocation to U.K.	20,50,65
	For Australia (Heavy)	71
	Force For India	65
	Force For Middle East	65
BRITISH DOMINIONS:	Representation Of	23
BURMA:	Air Transports For Forces	72
	Australian Troops For	43
	British Sphere Of Activity	44
	Employment Of A.V.G.	6,18,31
	General Alexander Takes Command Of British Forces	86
	Heavy Bombardment Squadrons From ABDA Area	53
	List of British Forces In India	89
	Reverts to India Command	43,58
	Supply And Maintenance of Air Forces	54
	Transport Aircraft For	135,143
	Transport Planes For	72
	Withdrawal Of British Forces	86
CASEY, Rt.Hon.R.G.:	Present At Meeting	57
CAUCASUS:	Defense Of	74
CEYLON:	Possibility Of Japanese Attack	88
CHIANG-KAI-SHEK:	Support Of	14

SUBJECT		PAGE NO.
CHINA:	Air Routes Into	144
	British Sphere Of Activity	44
	Employment Of A.V.G.	6,18,31
	Included In U.S. Sphere Of Strategic Control	103
	Proposal To Bolster Chinese Morale	40,51
	Transport Aircraft For	143
	U.S. Forces	6
	U.S. Obligation To Assist	54
COASTAL PATROLS:	Use Of Civilian Aircraft For	94
COLLABORATION:	Between United Nations	34
	Post Arcadia	9
COMBINED:	Intelligence	34
	Meteorological Committee, Charter For	67
	Military Transportation Committee, Charter For	35
COMMITTEES:	Arnold-Evill-Towers	122
	Combined Military Transportation Committee, Charter For	35
	Communications Board, Washington – Amendment of Directive	154
	Meteorological Committee, Charter For	67
	Munitions Assignments Board, Establishment Of	29
COMMUNICATIONS:	Adequacy for Universal Application	128,153
	Board, Washington – Amendment of Directive	154
	Rapid Military	128
CONVOYS:	Use of Great Circle Route	46
DIEGO SUAREZ:	Plan for Occupation	67

SUBJECT		PAGE NO.
DUTCH:	Additional Fighter Type Aircraft for N.E.I.	37
	Aircraft Allocated To Australia	114
	Forces In Java	54
	Forces Lost	86
	Representation Of	23
	Supplies For In The ABDA Area	10,16
	Take Over Command Of ABDA Area	62
	U.S. Aircraft Scheduled For Delivery	86
EASTERN FLEET:	Transfer Of British Submarines From ABDA Area	64
EGYPT:	Proposals For U.S. Air Units In Cairo	99
	U.S. Pursuit Squadrons To	64
EQUIPMENT:	For U.S. Divisions	107
	From Semi-Trained Units For Overseas Units	107
	Lack Of For U.S. Troops	73
ESCORT VESSELS:	U.S.-British Requirements	116
EUROPE:	Offensive Operations In	109
FIGHTER AIRCRAFT:	Additional For N.E.I.	37
	For Australia	124
	For India	124-125
FIJI:	Air Defense Of	64
FRENCH:	Free French Desire Command In New Caledonia	59
GAS:	German New Type	157
	Possibility of Use	145
GYMNAST:	Delay Due To Movement To North Ireland	30

VII

SUBJECT		PAGE NO.
GYMNAST: (Continued)	Modified Super	14
	Possibility Of	47
	Super	87
	Super, Shipping For	7
HAWAII:	Bases Between Australia And	44
HELFRICH, Admiral:	Commanding Combined Naval Forces in ABDA Area	39
ICELAND:	British Air Units Remain	105
	Command In	96,105
	Relief Of British Troops In	96,106,113,153
INDIA:	Air Transport Facilities	72
	British Sphere Of Activity	44
	Control Of Burma	43,58
	Fighter Type Aircraft For	124,125
	Japanese Intentions Against	88
	List Of British Forces To Withstand Attack From Burma	89
	Request For Transport Planes For	130
	Transport Aircraft For	135,143
INDIAN OCEAN:	Naval Bases In	77,98
	Situation In	132
INTELLIGENCE:	Combined	34
IRAQ:	German Capabilities In	120,154
IRELAND:	(See North Ireland)	
JAPAN:	Economical Employment Of Air Forces Against	35
	Expectancy Of Attack On Port Moresby	88
	Intentions Against India And Australia	88

VIII

SUBJECT		PAGE NO.
JAPAN: (Continued)	Possible Action Against Australia And New Zealand	25
	Russian Attitude To	19
	U.S. Air Attack On	153
JAPANESE THEATER OF WAR:	Distribution Of Naval Bases	35
	Distribution of Naval Forces	35
JAVA:	Distribution Of Dutch Forces	70
	Dutch Forces In	54
	Dutch Forces Lost	86
	Evacuation Of Forces	57
	Unsound To Reinforce	45
LANDING CRAFT:	Availability Of In August, 1942, and April, 1943	138
	Production Of Increased	125, 138
	Transportation In Atlantic	126
	U.S.-British Building Programs	117
MacARTHUR, General:	Appointment As Supreme Commander In Southwest Pacific Area	93
	Departure From Philippines	93
	Directive As Supreme Commander In Southwest Pacific Area	102
MADAGASCAR:	Plan For Occupation	67
MALAYA:	And New Guinea	16
MALAY BARRIER:	Disposition Of Naval Forces	61
MARSHALL, General:	Visit To London	132
MERCHANT SHIPPING:	Lack Of To Transport U.S. Troops	46
	Losses Of In Relation To War	45, 93
METEOROLOGICAL COMMITTEE:	Charter For	67

	SUBJECT	PAGE NO.
MIDDLE EAST:	Admiral Stark's Views On	89
	Forces Withdrawn For Far East And India	89
	Importance Of In Relation To U.K. And Far East	90
	Reinforcement Of Air Forces	95
	Situation In	89
MUNITIONS:	Assignments	107
	Assignments Board, Establishment Of	29
	Assignments, Directive For	107,139
	Assignments, Strategic Guidance For	92
	Ground Forces, Assignment Of	73
	Strategic Policy Regarding Assignment Of	73-74
NETHERLANDS EAST INDIES:	Additional Fighter Type Aircraft For	37
	U.S. Aircraft Allocated To	114,122
	U.S. Aircraft Scheduled For Delivery To	86
NEW CALEDONIA:	Command In	59,66
	Relief of U.S. Garrison By Australia	2
NEW GUINEA:	And Malaya	16
	Situation In	88
NEW ZEALAND:	Air Defense Of	64
	Air Requirements For	36
	British Allocation Of Pursuit Planes	26
	Possible Japanese Action Against	25,92
	Proposals Re Sphere Of Responsibility	78
	Pursuit Squadrons For	65
	Troops In Middle East	113
	Views Regarding Strategic Responsibility	112

	SUBJECT	PAGE NO.
NORTH IRELAND:	Move Of U.S. Troops To	29
	U.S. Troops For	96
OFFENSIVE:	Air, Against Enemy Bases, Yards, And Ships	155
	Air, Possibility Of Against England	145
	Operations In Europe	109
OPERATIONS:	Amphibious, Inspection by British Officers	109
	Continental, General Marshall's Visit To London	132
	Offensive, In Europe	109
PACIFIC:	War Council - London And Washington	103
	War Council - Relation To Southwest Pacific Area	98
PHILIPPINE AREA:	Japanese Landing In	145
	Supplies For	2,5
POLICY:	Strategic, Re Assignment Of Munitions	73-74
PORT MORESBY:	Expectancy Of Japanese Attack	88
POST ARCADIA:	Collaboration	9
PRESIDENT:	Proposals On Division Of Strategic Responsibility	97
PRIME MINISTER:	Message From On Current Situation.	77
	Proposed Presidential Reply To	79
PRIORITIES DIRECTIVE:	Study Of Production Of Critical Weapons	47

SUBJECT		PAGE NO.
PURSUIT AIRCRAFT:	Accompany Heavy Bombardment Groups To U.K.	50
	For Australia And New Zealand	65
	Planes For Middle East	65
	Requirements Of For European Air Offensive	144,148
	U.S. Squadrons To Egypt	64
RATAY, Colonel:	Predicts German Air Offensive	145
RUSSIA:	Allocation of Transports For	128
	Attitude to Japan	19
	Supplies To, Difficulty	131
SHIPPING:	Merchant Losses	93
SINGAPORE:	Prisoners Taken	48
SOUTHWEST PACIFIC AREA:	Directive For Supreme Commander	102
	Final Line of Demarkation with Indian Ocean Area	104
	Requisition of Material	140,143,149
	Tentative Arrangements For Commanders In	98
SPAATZ, General:	In London	150
SPHERE OF RESPON-SIBILITY:	British--Indian Ocean	70
	U.S.--Pacific Ocean	70
ST. PIERRE AND MIQUELON:	Coup d'etat	24
STRATEGIC AREAS:	Demarkation Of	70,71
STRATEGIC RESPON-SIBILITY:	Australian Views on For Pacific Area	102
	Draft Reply of President To Prime Minister	103

XII

SUBJECT		PAGE NO.
STRATEGIC RESPON- SIBILITY (Cont'd):	Of U.K. and U.S.--Directives To Supreme Commander	112
	President's proposals on Division Of	97
STRATEGY:	Concept as Guide for Allocation, Production, and Expansion	120
	U.S.--British Policy	120
SYRIA:	German Capabilities In	120,154
TAHITI:	Defense Of	8,9,15
TANKS:	Production And Requirements	49
TIMOR	Garrison For	2,31
TORRES STRAIT:	Proposal For Mining	39,48
TRANSPORT AIRCRAFT:	For Burma And India	135,143
	For China	143
	For India, Request For	130
	General Allocations	130
TRANSPORTATION:	Combined Military Transportation Committee, Charter For	35
	Of Troops On Cargo Vessels	137
TROOPS:	Air Borne -- Expansion And Training	130
	Air Borne - Participation In Commando Raids	130
	Transportation Of On Cargo Vessels	137
TURKEY:	German Capabilities In	120
UNITED NATIONS:	Aircraft Allocation Of	150
	Aircraft Production Of	37

	SUBJECT	PAGE NO.
UNITED NATIONS (Continued):	Aircraft Resources Of	121
	War Collaboration Between	34
VAN MOOK, Dr. H.E.:	Present at Meeting	27
VICHY FRANCE:	Possessions in Caribbean	141
	Relations With	24
WEST AFRICAN AIR ROUTE:	Defense Of	49
WESTERN ATLANTIC AREA:	Change In As Defined In ABC-1	8,40

www.ingramcontent.com/pod-product-compliance
Lightning Source LLC
Chambersburg PA
CBHW08083823 0426
43665CB00021B/2876